A Rainbow Book

The Bliss
of
Becoming One!

Integrating "Feminine" Feelings
Into the Male Psyche
Mainstreaming the
Gender Community

Rachel Miller

Rainbow Books, Inc.

Library of Congress Cataloging-in-Publication Information

Miller, Rachel, 1941-
    The bliss of becoming one! : integrating feminine feelings into the male psyche :
mainstreaming the gender community   Rachel Miller.
        p.   cm.
    Includes bibliographical references.
    ISBN 1-56825-031-2 (alk. paper)
    1. Transvestism. 2. Gender identity. 3. Men--Psychology.
    4. Clothing and dress--Psychological aspects. I. Title.
    HQ77.M55 1996
    305.3--dc20   95-25566
                                                                        CIP

The Bliss of Becoming One!
Integrating "Feminine" Feelings into the Male Psyche
Mainstreaming the Gender Community
Copyright 1996 © Opportunities for Improvement

Published by Rainbow Books, Inc.
Editorial Offices
P. O. Box 430
Highland City, FL 33846-0430 USA
Telephone Fax (941) 648-4420
e-mail: NAIP@aol.com
Orders: Telephone (800) 356-9315, Fax (800) 242-0036

Cover interior design by Betsy A. Lampé
Cover graphic design by Howard Evan Weintraub (used with permission)

Disclaimer

The ideas presented in this book are not intended as advice or recommendations in any particular case and do not in any way substitute for professional counseling and personal judgment. This book should not be used as a manual for self-diagnosis or self-treatment, since such diagnosis and treatment are potentially dangerous.

Not all self-help ideas are suitable for everyone. Actions based on the ideas contained in this or any other book on self-help may result in unexpected events. To reduce the risk of such unexpected events, seek professional counsel from a psychiatrist, psychologist or other licensed therapist before taking actions.

The writer, publisher and distributors of this book disclaim any liabilities or loss in connection with the ideas contained herein. It is almost certainly in your best interest to find a responsible and caring professional, who will work with you and guide the course of your actions. You are urged to allow the professional to know your personal status thoroughly and to assist in prescribing appropriate actions for your particular situation.

Manufactured in the United States of America.

Dedication

Dear Mom,

You are a wonderful lady, and I appreciate you more each day. Until I showed you this book, you didn't know about my deepest secret of transvestism. Since you didn't know about this facet of me, it may seem odd to dedicate this book to you. I have come to realize that you have provided me with continuous love, support and understanding. Without you standing by me as a person, I would not have been able to face this issue, much less write this book. Maybe men have to grow up before they can appreciate their mothers. Maybe that's why, like so many others, I want to simply say, "Thanks, Mom. I love you."

Your Son

Acknowledgments

I can never fully repay my debt to all those who helped me, but consider this a down payment. Of those who helped, three deserve special praise:

My wife and best friend. She always makes my life better. She had no idea about my transvestism when we married. When I told her, she was extremely supportive. It was through her encouragement that I started writing this book. She adopted the role of loving realist, and she keeps me on track. There is no one else I'd rather spend my life with. She is the best thing that ever happened to me.

Tracy was my first cross-dressing correspondent. We became friends and shared many aspects of each other's lives. Tracy understood what I was going through and the positive reinforcement I needed. There was always acceptance, never guilt. He brought me through the critical first six months of facing the issues. The frequent letters were filled with feeling, depth and understanding. That experience was an essential ingredient in my quest for wholeness.

Vivian Allen. On two separate occasions, Vivian provided the guidance to take a manuscript, which I thought was finished, to a higher level. Every reader benefits from the new and improved version.

Contents

The Hook

> "We don't need to be creative for most of what we do, but when there is a need to 'think something different,' our own attitudes can get in the way. I call these attitudes 'mental locks.'
>
> "Mental locks can be opened in one of two ways. The first technique is to become aware of them, and then to temporarily forget them when you are trying to generate ideas. If that doesn't work, maybe you need a 'whack on the side of the head.' That should dislodge the presuppositions that hold the locks in place."
>
> –Roger von Oech, author
> *A Whack On the Side of the Head*

Why Read This Book?

When faced with something new, the normal reaction is to ask, "What's in it for me?" You want to receive value for your investment of time and money. So, why should you read this book? It has three target audiences. Each audience has its own unique perspective. Each will receive its own unique value. Which one describes you best?

1 — If you have no connection to the gender community [1]
this book is designed to assist you in
— gaining an appreciation of our pain and suffering
— understanding that we have the same fundamental wants, needs
  and desires that you have
— recognizing that men have repressed their feelings and emotions
— realizing that we're not sexual deviants, and there is no reason to
  fear or avoid us
— learning that most ideas about appropriate male/female clothing
  and actions are arbitrary
— seeing that, by eliminating these restrictions, we could shed our
  unbearable burdens
— becoming more supportive of those who appear different.

2 — If you know someone in the gender community
this book will take you a step farther. It will show you that loved ones
hold the key to making it safe to reveal deeply buried secrets. A
man's *transvestite* [2] tendencies are buried more deeply than anything
else. You can be the catalyst to help a loved one break out of the
closet. You might even experience an additional bonus. Women are
disappointed in relationships where males are reluctant to engage in
intimacy. As a group, transvestites tend to be more sensitive than
typical males. Therefore, you can help create the deep, loving relationship you desire by understanding, accepting and encouraging
your sensitive transvestite.

3 — If you are a member of the gender community
this book will improve your life, if you are willing to change. It pro-
motes health, wholeness and unity. It demonstrates constructive
changes that will benefit you. It describes a shared vision that is specific enough to embrace your needs, yet general enough to include

---

[1] The group of males and females personally affected by any gender issues
such as androgeny, cross-dressing, transgenderism, transsexualism or transvestism.
[2] A person who wears clothing usually associated with persons of the opposite sex.

everyone. It encourages you to create your own personal style — a picture of how you want to look and act.

Striving for that personal style can be a powerful motivation to achieve your goals. This book explains proven techniques for changing an unacceptable current reality into the desired, shared vision. It invites you to see difficult issues as opportunities for improvement, instead of problems. It exposes flaws in the arguments that are used to try to convince you that you are somehow unfit. It assists in breaking down sexual and emotional stereotypes which can prevent you from reaching a clearer understanding of yourself. It shows that change is within your grasp. It endorses a simple, yet effective method for implementing change — the Golden Rule. It describes the steps of accepting, sharing, helping and educating that serve as guideposts on your quest towards wholeness. The same steps set the stage for transforming society. This book discusses the considerations in each step to help you determine their appropriateness in your life. Finally, it urges you to join a movement to bring us into the mainstream of society.

If you want to better understand and accept
your gender feelings and actions,
this book will help you accomplish that goal.

If you want your loved ones to more fully accept
your gender feelings and actions,
this book will help you work with them.

If you want to help others in your community,
this book provides encouragement.

If you want to make the world more open to you,
this book provides the framework.

Be Creative — Give It a Chance

The concept of opening mental locks is extremely important in how you approach this book. Suppose I say the word *clock*. Most people immediately see an image that reflects their perspective of a clock. Images of a wall clock, an alarm clock or a time clock are perfectly valid, but suppose the image I intend is Big Ben as seen through the view-finder of a camera. Suppose I say that a major consideration in taking a picture of the clock, is to see enough of the clock while still being able to tell what time it is. If you envision one of the other images, my statement seems nonsensical. You might conclude that I don't know what I'm talking about. You might dismiss what I say because my words fail to match your image.

When I present an idea, you will see an image based on your perspective. If I challenge your perceptions, offer seemingly impractical or implausible advice, use a writing manner or words that you dislike or don't address a topic the way you would, you might conclude that I don't know what I'm talking about. You might reject the idea because my words fail to match your image. That would be a bad approach even if everything were fine; but, everything is most decidedly not fine. You know that the gender community has deeply rooted problems. Disregarding a potential solution simply because it doesn't exactly match your image wouldn't qualify you for the wisest-person-of-the-year award.

The past and present views have taken us forward great distances. A new, revitalized view of the future is needed to reach the next plateau. Give yourself the gift of a special opportunity and take a good look at this new view. Be creative and alert for mental locks in this adventure. You will discover things here that vary from your perception of the world. Don't let that discovery become an obstruction. Don't abandon your perspective, just set it aside for awhile. If you reject the new view because it is different, you will lose all of the benefits and the rest of us will lose your valuable contributions. All of us lose. Instead, give it a chance so that everyone can win. Rather than getting whacked on the side of the head, open your mental locks and combine the new view with your existing one. Dr. von Oech's book is an excellent stimulus for breaking out of our normal thinking patterns.

How About Those Who Aren't Transvestites?

There is another extremely important concept in how you approach this book. There are great differences within our community.

Those differences are often used to classify us into sub-groups that serve to divide us. Subscribers to this divisive approach would place me in the heterosexual, male *cross-dresser* [3] sub-group. They would have you believe that my words can only apply to other members of my sub-group. *Wrong!* While that classification helps *define* me, it does not accurately *describe* me. It also does not limit the truth of what I have to say. Because of my background, I have greater empathy for those who consider themselves cross-dressers. We have experienced similar feelings and lived similar lives, thus there is a stronger connection. If you see yourself in a role other than a cross-dresser, I cannot relate to your situation as well because we don't share the same background. However, that does not invalidate these principles nor my intent to join all of us. The principles are universal and extend beyond our community. Regardless of how you visualize yourself, look objectively at the issues and principles. We have much more in common to unite us than differences to separate us. We need each other because our future well-being is connected. We can't afford to create or maintain sub-groups based on our differences. Neither can society.

How Will It Work?

I will share my feelings and experiences to encourage you to take similar steps to improve your life. My pledge is to be open and honest in order to earn your trust and confidence. By the time you finish, you will recognize my commitment to the proverb:

> "A good man is known by his truthfulness;
> A false man by deceit and lies."

> — *Proverbs*, Chapter 12, Verse 17 [4]

My principles and beliefs are clearly identified throughout. You

---

[3] An alternate term for transvestite.

[4] All Biblical quotations are taken from *The Living Bible, Paraphrased* published by Tyndale House Publishers, Inc. Wheaton, IL

may agree with some and disagree with others, but it is crucial that you develop your own. They will carry you forward on your quest. Segments will push you to examine issues and record your thoughts. It is important that you take the time to do so. You will derive maximum value by becoming actively involved and working through the issues. By remaining passive, change will not occur, and you will receive little value.

> "Change — real change — comes from the inside out. It doesn't come from hacking at the leaves of attitude and behavior with quick fix personality ethic techniques. It comes from striking at the root — the fabric of our thought, the fundamental, essential paradigms, which give definition to our character and create the lens through which we see the world."

> — Stephen R. Covey
> *The 7 Habits of Highly Effective People*

We are embarking on an adventure of change. Dr. Covey tells us that real change starts within ourselves. Accomplishing our shared vision requires us to learn to see and act differently, but remember:

> "You should probably never make wholesale revisions to your way of thinking . . . Rather, you should revisit your beliefs when it seems appropriate, and modify them carefully and a little bit at a time. Never change a belief based on someone else's word, no matter who they may be. They could be wrong or, worse, lying. Don't you dare change any of your beliefs based on what you read here! If an idea here seems worth integrating into your view of the world, first try it out and see if it works for you. If it does, then, and only then, integrate it into your system of beliefs."

> — Nancy Reynolds Nangeroni
> *Building Bridges,*
> *Coming Out With A Plumb*

Will It Be Easy?

We like our reading easy and relaxing but reading this book will be hard and disturbing. We like to be spectators and not get involved, but this book will drag you out of your seat and onto the playing field. We don't like to face difficult things, but this book pushes you to face issues. We like a nice sugar-coating, but this book cuts through sugar-coating with truth. We procrastinate, but this book calls for immediate action. We like products to entice us with the silver-bullet promise of a quick fix, but silver bullets are for the Lone Ranger and vampires, and there is no quick fix. You know that anything as important as achieving your goals requires time and effort. The good news is that you are capable of making these changes, and there are many resources to help you succeed.

My Background

I have been a transvestite as long as I can remember. That condition brought with it a great deal of pain and suffering. I have experienced low self-esteem, shame, fear of rejection, isolation — all sorts of negative emotions. I was not emotionally healthy and didn't see any path for conditions to improve. I was on a treadmill, unable to move forward. In absolute desperation, I determined to find relief, regardless of how it turned out. When that quest for relief started, I had no plan, only an overwhelming need for relief.

To an outside observer I had it made. I had a great wife and loving family. I had a beautiful home with all of the amenities. I was a skilled professional with a high-paying job in a prestigious company. I was an active member in my local church. What more could anyone ask? Even with all those good things seemingly filling my life, I was constantly pretending not to be myself. *I liked women's clothes.* Showing that interest wasn't acceptable. Consequently, I pretended not to care about those things. Each time I denied my feelings, I felt terrible. It was like constantly admitting that I was not good enough. That denial crossed into each area of my life and ate away those pleasures like a cancerous growth. It was the unacceptable pain of remaining in that state of self-denial that ultimately overcame my fear of finding the truth.

I started my quest trembling with fear and doubt. I found a copy of the *TV/TS Tapestry Journal* in an X-rated book store. My heart was pounding as I flipped the pages. In that sleazy place, I found the first positive publication about transvestites that I had ever seen. It seemed too good to be true, yet I almost walked out without it. How could a respectable man in a business suit buy this, this . . . stuff? It took a few minutes to gather enough courage, but the possibility of finding help overpowered my fears. I bought the magazine.

In *Tapestry* I found an ad for books by Virginia Prince that seemed to apply to my situation. I wanted to get them, but how? I certainly couldn't have them sent to work or my home. What could I do? I noticed that most addresses in *Tapestry* were post office boxes. Could I get a post office box? Sure. But, wait a minute. They'll want my *real* name. Maybe I could use my name, but then say I'm sharing the box with another person. That should work. With exceptionally sweaty palms I opened a box in my name. I selected the female name Rachel Miller, and notified the post office that she would also receive mail there. I ordered the books and checked the box frequently. Each time I was certain that everybody in the place knew I was a transvestite and that they were watching and laughing. But no one ever said anything. The books arrived, and I slipped off to a secluded spot to drink in the contents. In the books I found people like me, men who enjoyed wearing women's clothing. I should have realized that I wasn't so unusual, but somehow it had seemed to me that only perverts would do the things I did. That reading reassured me and helped me to begin to feel better about myself.

I read the personal ads in the magazine and wondered what those people were like. The magazine provided a confidential method of correspondence. Why not try it? I spent two weeks drafting a letter that described my situation, carefully excluding any facts that could identify me. I selected several cross-dressers who appeared to be interesting correspondents. I even picked one whose picture projected an extremely sexy appearance. It took all the courage I could muster to mail the letters. One last deep breath and . . . now they are in the US Mail, and I cannot back down. My God, it was hard to breathe.

Mailing the letters was a breeze compared to facing the replies. One day I slipped into the post office, opened the door to my little mail box and *voilà*, there was a letter. It was addressed to Rachel Miller. Hey, that's *me*. Once again, air was having a difficult time getting inside my body. Maybe I didn't have to open the letter. After all, I had already done a lot. Couldn't I quit here? No! I opened the letter and knew that I could never go back. The genie had escaped. In the letter I found someone who understood my fears and feelings, someone who accepted and supported me, someone who shattered the feelings of guilt and shame. What followed was an intense, six-month period of frenzied letter writing with several correspondents. They became my windows to an unfamiliar world, therapists in my quest for health. I found out I wasn't alone. I found out I wasn't a bad person. I found out there was hope. I began to find relief.

In time my fears began to mutate into growing feelings of self-confidence. I felt good enough about myself to finally tell my wife the truth about my transvestism. It was a difficult step, but taking it removed a tremendous burden. I no longer had to sneak around trying to get a small taste of cross-dressing. I quit hiding my clothes and moved them into our closet. I began wearing my sexiest outfits to bed on a regular basis. At times I got completely dressed and made-up, and my wife and I spent the evening together. Our sex life improved. My life began showing dramatic gains by coming out of the closet. The cancerous growth was retreating.

A friend sent me a Boulton & Park Society survey on gender-related activities. It prompted me to examine how I felt, what I believed and what I wanted. As I was daydreaming about cross-dressing, an idea popped into my head. It wasn't much of an idea at first, but it grew and matured. I was dreaming about my ideal situation. In my dream, I lived in a world where men dressed and behaved in exactly the same manner that women did — and nobody cared. Gradually, I realized that it was possible to make that dream come true if others adopted it. Previously, I had only wanted to wear something feminine. I wasn't interested in helping any cause. Now, I saw a better future life for me. When others became committed, their lives would become better, too. So, partly out of self-interest and partly out of a desire to help others, I began to work towards that exciting future. My wife encouraged me to record my impressions, and they developed into this book.

The Movement

My ultimate purpose is twofold: The first is to encourage you to integrate all of your traits into a complete person; the second is to prod the entire gender community to join in a movement to bring us into the mainstream of society. Both the integration of traits and the movement will have a positive impact on your quality of life, whether you are an integral part of the community, know someone in it or are not connected to it. True success will occur when you join in and experience great joy and happiness as you discover —

The Bliss of Becoming One!

What If . . . ?

"Our life is what our thoughts make it."

—Marcus Aurelius

Let's Play A Game . . .

that is fun, easy and has no right or wrong answers. There are only winners, and it doesn't require any special knowledge or skill. You don't need to practice, because you are already the world's greatest expert. No one can play the game better than you, and no one could possibly get more out of playing the game than you. It will exercise your creativity and help make you a big winner in this adventure.

As a child I remember sitting in a darkened kitchen, hunched over the radio, listening to *Inner Sanctum*. The creaky door opened, the mysterious voice spoke and my imagination sent me racing off into another world. Use the power of your imagination to envision a world that will make you healthier and happier. Involve all of your senses: sight, smell, touch, taste and hearing. The more senses that you use, the more you will gain.

In high school I was a science fiction addict and read the magazine *What If.* The stories began with a premise that was usually far-fetched. If you accepted the premise, the rest of the story was logical, consistent and could happen. To make sense out of my desires to cross-dress, I developed my own premise. This one isn't as far-fetched as it might first appear. The rest of the story is logical, consistent and could happen. All you have to do is relax, grab a cold drink, plunk down in your favorite chair and —

Play . . .

The Premise

What if . . .
you lived in a society where it was impossible to distinguish men from women based on their clothing, hair style, jewelry, makeup or behavior patterns?

What if . . .
there were no sexual or gender judgments attached to wearing dresses or pants? Everyone wore what they liked and felt comfortable wearing, each fashion statement was politically correct and no one cared what you wore, or how you acted, as long as you did not harm others.

What if . . .
the terms cross-dresser, transgendered, transsexual and transvestite, became unimportant and disappeared? Discussions about them melted away and everyone simply became a person, being themselves, without pretenses.

What if . . .
the sexual preference stereotypes sometimes associated with being bisexual, heterosexual or homosexual stopped being an issue? Everyone simply defined their own sexuality and no negative connotations were attached to any of the choices.

What if . . .
that open society actually existed?

Have I gone too far with my premise? The evidence says no. Have you noticed that what is considered acceptable apparel and behavior is constantly changing? Have you considered that it will continue to change whether people want it to or not? This premise describes one possible outcome for the coming changes. It may not be the most likely outcome, but it is certainly *possible*. Perhaps, if pressure were applied, that outcome would become more likely. For now, suspend judgment, accept the premise and dream along with me.

My Personal Style

As the picture of this ideal society developed, it occurred to me that it was the answer I had been seeking. In such a world, I could experiment with dressing in novel ways without pretending to be a woman, and without fear of being found out or laughed at. Given a free choice, would I select a suit, a tightly buttoned, white-cotton shirt and a tie to wear? Certainly not! I find that men's clothing is often dull, unimaginative and uncomfortable, while women have fabulous options. Check the catalogs and compare. Yes, I admit to being just a teeny bit jealous. Well, why can't we have those options? There are days when I want to wear plain, casual clothes. I don't want the hassle of dressing up each morning, but I would like to several times a week. Rather than continuing to grumble about the misfortunes associated with men's clothing, I decided to create a look that I liked. I discovered that by developing my own appearance, the premise became more real and more important for me. I started to dream about how I would look in that open society and what fashion statements I would make.

I've always considered myself a leg man and find myself drawn more to women's legs than any other part of the body. Okay, I do look at other parts, but I am a leg man. I'm tall and slender, well, pretty slender, and running helps keep my legs in shape. Even my mother-in-law said I have good legs. The question is, how can I best emphasize my legs? That was fun to answer.

Skirt – My first choice is short skirts. I like numerous fashions: straight, pleated, soft, sheer, ruffled, flounced . . . With a body like mine, it's much easier to find a skirt than a dress that fits. I do have a problem fitting into fashionable clothing. I like the hem above the knee to show my legs while I have legs to show. I'm beginning to understand women's preoccupation with aging. Ugh. Look at those ugly veins.

High Heels – I enjoy high heels. *Enjoy* isn't exactly the right term. Actually, I am infatuated with high heels. Flats and short, squatty heels have never appealed to me. A 3- or 4-inch heel works well, but I also have a pair of super-tall, 5-inch, spiked heels. Trying to walk in those is quite an experience. I found a local store that carries a wide variety of attractive shoes that fit comfortably. That store is a gift because a sexy-looking, size-13 wide isn't that easy to find.

Silky Stockings – I love the look, feel and sound of soft, sheer, silky stockings. Forget that stretchy yarn used in certain stockings. Why not get burlap bags? They feel crummy and have zero sex-appeal. I used to hate panty hose, but have discovered some that are not only delightful, but also practical when wearing a short skirt.

With the skirt, high heels and silky stockings, my leg treatment is mostly settled, but what about the rest of me? I like soft, sheer blouses, and again in various fashions. I am especially fond of lace collars, appliqués, sheer material and other frilly details. I have long arms and have trouble finding long-sleeved blouses that fit decently. With my hyper-metabolism short sleeves are more practical, but I still love long sleeves.

I like relatively long fingernails, though not long enough to interfere with my computer keyboard. I admire bright red polish, but I'm not certain that red is one of my colors. Toenails are another matter entirely, and I'm indifferent about doing anything with them.

Hair was difficult until recently. I don't like wigs and have a large head (no wise cracks). Even the larger wigs are tight and uncomfortable, and the more I dress the more importance I attach to comfort. I wanted to emphasize my naturally wavy hair, but I have a dandruff problem and must shampoo frequently with fairly harsh products. I also hate the smell of the permanent solution used in salons. Because of those factors, I considered long hair with fancy curls to be impractical. That was a disappointing discovery but an answer was on the way My niece and nephew had planned a Billy Joel party, and my wife suggested styling my hair the way he does, medium length and brushed back. I tried it, and it's a winner. Many people have commented enthusiastically. I like it, can wear it daily and it can be perfected over time. It was a solid step in creating my style.

Defining my makeup is spotty, and that is exactly the right term, *spotty* makeup. I enjoy lipstick, generally in bright red shades to match my nails. I like blush on my cheeks but not too dark or heavy. I am experimenting with light touches in the hopes of creating high cheek bones. Look out Sophia Loren. I like dark shadow and outlined eyes, but I don't know how to do it without looking like a Halloween leftover. I have tried liquid makeup and don't like it at all. I'm not sure if I want to use a powder. I did find one product that covers skin blemishes like magic. Obviously this area is a gigantic opportunity for improvement.

In the past I never admitted that I liked jewelry. I was afraid it would unveil my secret desires. The truth is, I do like jewelry and have a natural tendency toward more expensive items. Big surprise! I prefer gold, and my wife bought me a beautiful bracelet that is a unisex style. She also helped me select a diamond ring. Now I sit around reflecting sunlight off the stone. Sound familiar? I like earrings, but I restrict myself to clip-ons since I'm too chicken to pierce my ears. I like pearls too, and made what appeared to be a casual comment to my wife; perhaps for Christmas dear. It worked, and she bought me two pairs. It was fun to turn the tables and use the same, not-so-subtle tricks on my wife. This jewelry thing is great, but I hope I don't run out of money.

I decided that I wouldn't wear fake boobs, undergo electrolysis (I have a light beard and am generally not hairy), speak in a higher voice, take hormones or try to act effeminate. I have no significant desire to do those things. I just want to be myself. Most of all, I want to drop my dual names. I adopted the *femme* name, Rachel Miller, to protect my identity. While corresponding with other cross-dressers, I realized that I was treating Rachel as a separate person. As I became healthier, I understood that Rachel was an integral part of me. I use the name for security but look forward to the day when that won't be necessary.

How Would You Do It?

Creating your look is essential to success in this process. It is a wonderfully exciting technique for turning the general vision into one that *matters* to you. Ask yourself, "How would I look if there were no constraints?" What would you like to wear if there were no need to worry about passing or being read?

Today many seem to feel that there are only two choices: look totally like a man or look totally like a woman. Do you feel that if you don't employ a complete, woman's image, you'll be laughed at? That may be true *now*, but you are dreaming of an entirely different world. Set aside how things are and dream of *how you want them to be*. Maybe you want to dress as — a business woman or a hooker or a housewife. Maybe you want to have large breasts, speak in a higher pitched voice or walk like an Egyptian. Remember, in this open society no one cares what you wear or how you act. You are free to choose whatever you like. Would you be 100% feminine? Would you mix and match with some parts obviously feminine and others obviously masculine? Would you go in drag or in drab? Would you indulge and pamper yourself with bubble baths, manicures, massages? The possibilities are endless, and you can start now by closing your eyes and using all of your senses to dream of

— the soft, gentle touch of cool silk against your skin.
— the subtle aroma of your favorite fragrance wafting into your nostrils.
— the rich, creamy taste of luscious lipstick on your lips.
— the wonderful, whooshing sound of nylon stockings brushing against your satin slip.
— the sensational look of the exquisite lace of your best, sheer blouse.
— the sensuous, ecstatic feeling that comes from knowing that under your standard issue men's clothing, your entire body is being caressed by the sexiest, filmiest, Parisian lingerie.

That was an example of using all of your senses to enrich the experience. Did you enjoy it? To get the most out of this book, *involve all of your senses. Read* aloud to hear the words. Imagine how things would *look, taste, feel, smell.* Write your answers to the questions. Act out the situations. Do whatever you can to get fully involved in the process.

As you take the time to define your appearance, you will begin to receive value. So let's get started right now. How would you look if there were no constraints? Remember you want the truth for yourself, not what you think others want. Whatever you decide is okay. Ask yourself,

"What is my personal style?"
Where Is This Going?

What kind of clothing would you like to wear?
How would you do your hair style?
What kind of jewelry do you like?
How would you do your makeup?
What behavior patterns do you like?
Under what circumstances would you like to dress?
How often do you want to dress?
What else is important to you?

You've embraced the premise of an open society where all individuals can dress and act the way they want without any indication of sex or gender. You've created a style that is uniquely yours and reflects how you want to look and act. You might wonder, *Where is this going?* I must confess that this is more than a harmless little game. This seemingly innocent game actually has incredible power to transform things, and by playing it you have laid the foundation to accomplish the changes you've been dreaming about.

The game is based on a model described by Peter Senge in *The Fifth Discipline*. In that model the shared vision is a specific destination to achieve. You have made the vision more real by adding your own unique, personal style. Together they form a picture of a desired future, a future that has intrinsic value for you. The picture is not vague but a tangible, individual vision that *matters*. It is a clear picture of where you want to be and how things will look and feel when you get there. The shared vision is the desired objective, and the current reality is the present condition. There is usually a large gap between the two. In this case the gap looks like the space between the solar system and the rim of the Milky Way, (the galaxy, not the candy bar). A large gap can lead to discouragement and a lowering of the vision, but it can also generate creative tension — a powerful force for improvement. Visualize creative tension as a giant rubber band, capable of pulling us forward through the gap. It is able to do exactly that.

This book is designed to encourage you to make the changes that will benefit you, our community and everybody. Encouragement gives hope, confidence and support to others. Everyone needs that because making these changes does take courage. Facing and dealing with things recognized as dangerous, difficult or painful — instead of withdrawing from them — is a courageous act. But taking these steps brings great rewards, and you don't want to let anything prevent you from achieving those dreams.

You took the first step by embracing the shared vision and creating your personal style. That willingness to adopt another approach is the key to success. Nothing important happens without a vision. One person's vision has power, but a *shared* vision has significantly greater power. None of us can achieve it alone, but together we can. Each of us has unique ways to open the closed society, and that variety adds to our strength. Your actions encourage others to join, which causes our collective power to increase dramatically. Open your mind to these new thoughts, release the creative tension and allow it to propel you forward to —

Shared Vision – An Open Society

Your Personal Style

Current Reality – A Closed Society

Convert your dreams into reality!

But

"Nothing in the world can take the place of persistence.
Talent will not; nothing is more common
than unsuccessful men with talent.
Genius will not; unrewarded genius is almost a proverb.
Education will not; the world is full of educated derelicts.
Persistence and determination alone are omnipotent."

—Calvin Coolidge

It's Impossible

You've seen an enticing picture of the future and so far it is a piece of cake. Guess what's next — the "current reality" crowd telling you that these changes are impossible. This is a good place to begin generating creative tension. There are those who will stand in your path, and you might even believe some of them. There must be compelling reasons why things are like this; after all, isn't "the system" designed in our best interest? Don't the people in charge always do what's best for us? Aren't they right when they tell us it's impossible to alter the system? If that's true, we can quit now and return to our constricting little closets.

But it's not true. The sum of all "valid" reasons for discriminating against us would fit comfortably in a thimble. We don't have to stay in those constricting closets any longer. There *aren't* any compelling reasons for how things are, and the system *isn't* designed in our interest. Our leaders *don't* always do what's most advantageous for us, and we do have the power to modify present conditions.

You don't need me to convince you which statements are true. Too often we don't give ourselves credit for being able to question things and think through issues. A TV (that's television not transvestite) evangelist used to say, "You don't have to check your brains at the door to be a good Christian." Often we assume the other person knows what he is talking about, decide we're no experts, and we take whatever he says as true. *That is a bad idea.* Don't trust the establishment to tell you whether you can change things. The establishment is in control. They don't want change because it could cause them to *lose* control. They tell us what works for them and try to convince us that it works for us. Hogwash! A basic law of human nature is that once established, an organization's primary goal is survival. It's a good thing to keep in mind. If they are wrong in how they treat us — and they are — do you think they will tell us they are wrong? Sorry. At best they will need a lot of prodding from us.

What Is the Favorite Word of a Five-year Old?

Since the establishment isn't telling us the truth, nor doing what's best for us, we're going to have to do a little thinking and questioning on our own. Thinking and questioning aren't hard, we just need practice. What follows is a practice exercise to perfect those skills. We have the native ability to become expert thinkers and questioners. Think of a five-year old. What do they do almost as second nature? They ask, "Why?" They are naturally inquisitive. They want to know how everything works and why. At times they take the concept to an extreme. We don't want extremism, but important concepts need to be challenged periodically to ensure their continued validity. Sometimes a concept was wrong from the beginning. Sometimes conditions have reversed, and it no longer makes sense. Sometimes it will be reaffirmed. In any case, every concept benefits from an occasional challenge. Each of us was once a five-year old, so we have the ability. Now, we need to exercise our ability.

My profession is computer system analysis and design. When presenting a new design concept to a veteran employee, the initial response is usually, "That will never work."

I ask, "Why?"

"Because we do it this way."

I ask the next logical question, "Why?"

The response is clearly intended to be the end of the conversation, "Because we've *always* done it *this* way."

Before getting thrown out, I have learned to shift from a discussion of why we do it like this, to why can't we do it another way. I might say, "Tell me why we can't try the new method? What would happen? What would be the problem?" They often bring up excellent issues that must be addressed, but the tone has shifted from defending the old, established order to finding techniques to make the new approach work.

We need a similar approach. We need to stop defending the established order and focus on making the new idea work. Asking, "Why?" is helpful in *challenging* how things are, but it tends to get bogged down in the past. It surfaces the arguments used to support the past. We need to learn when to transition to asking, "Why not?" which tends to focus on the future where effort can be devoted to making improvements. And for the record, our future is the future. Pretty profound, hey?

You understand that if you do nothing, the established order will continue unaltered. By starting to read this book, you indicated dissatisfaction with society. You don't want the established order to win by default. Do you? Of course not. Now hold onto your positive thoughts, because the next thing you will hear is the bad news as —

The Established Order Rains On Your Parade

"You can't dress like that. You can't act like that. You can't associate with real men. You are all weird. You ought to be ashamed of yourselves.

"You are all perverts. You are either homosexuals, or transsexuals, or transvestites and trying to be like girls. You sissies. You should all be locked up.

"Even the Bible says you are wrong. It says not to wear women's clothes. What's wrong with you?

"You can't tell your wife. You can't tell your family. You can't tell your friends. Nobody wants to be around people like you. If anyone finds out, you'll lose your wife, your job, everything.

"You better stay in that closet. You can only sneak around late at night with other weird characters like yourself. Even then you'd better not let us catch you, or you'll be sorry. We are going to laugh at you, ridicule you, beat you and chase you back into the closet where you belong.

"You thought it was cute to dream. You thought somehow you could transform the world. This is reality. It will always be like this. Get used to it. *Give up!*"

You have heard versions of that outburst. The people who make statements like that usually operate from an extremely negative, stereotypical view, and they assume that you fit that stereotype. You know better.

How Would You Describe the Differences?

Suppose you asked someone to describe the difference between members of the gender community and other people? Would you consider them reasonable if they tried to answer this question in one simple sentence? Would you consider those who took that approach uninformed, naive or purposefully unkind? Would you want your life summed up in one sweeping statement? It is impossible to interpret the life of a member of any group of people in that manner. Words like always and never are rarely accurate. It is much more accurate to use words like *most, some* or *seldom*. Many people want sweeping statements, but those generalizations create human zoos where you become a spectacle. Haven't you had more than enough of that?

There is a fundamental truth about stereotypical viewpoints — they are inaccurate. Telling the truth requires a balanced perspective of any group. Keep that in mind the next time someone dismisses you with an unbalanced statement.

Each of us is different. Some differences are more obvious than others, but we all have them. By certain standards we are all outsiders. After casting out everyone who doesn't meet a certain standard, who would be left? We need to learn to recognize and accept our differences. That is a valuable lesson for all.

This book concentrates on positive actions to improve the current reality. We all know that living in a closed society isn't a satisfying existence. The good news is that for the most part, the perceptions of us are wrong, and we can fix them. The quotation opening this chapter should encourage us to work through the process. It is popular because it applies to all of us. Some of us may lack certain skills. Some of us may lack great intelligence. Some of us may lack an extensive formal education, but each of us can exercise persistence. Therefore each of us can be successful. We say we want to solve our problems, but can't because we lack _____ (fill in the blank). If we want to solve our problems, we simply need to start work, and we need to have the persistence and determination to see our work through to completion. The question is not, "Can our problems be solved?" Of course they can be solved. The question is, "Are we willing to go to work and finish the job?"

"Today's hardship
leads to rewards in later life."

— Chinese Fortune Cookie

Fortune cookies sometimes provide a clear insight into life. Isn't it time for you to quit complaining and making excuses and —

Go to work and finish the job!

Why Not?

"You see things that are and say, 'Why?'
But I dream things that never were and say, 'Why not?'"

— George Bernard Shaw

It's An Opportunity

Was that previous outburst too harsh? You can try to hide from those storms under your umbrella, but you know it won't work. Many people would voice similar feelings if confronted by you in your finest regalia. Understanding? Not likely. Most people need an attitude check regarding gender-related issues. Now you could view this situation as a problem, or you could view it as an opportunity for improvement. Let's consider it an opportunity.

Why Is it Like This?

Suppose you were asked, "What sex is your shirt?" It wouldn't take long to assert that clothing doesn't have sex. It is neither male nor female. But what if the question were, "What gender is your shirt?" Does the same answer apply? Is a shirt masculine or feminine? Neither. Clothing doesn't have gender either; yet in today's culture, most people consider a shirt masculine because it is traditionally worn by males. Clothing itself has little to do with sex or gender. Ask yourself what makes a shirt intrinsically different from a blouse. Is it the material? The style? Having buttons on the opposite side? None of the above. There is no difference and no reason to consider one masculine and the other feminine.

Women wear tailored shirts without anyone raising an eyebrow, so why are people upset when a man wears a blouse? The answer is, *Currently accepted custom!* Custom is the primary factor in dictating who wears what. Custom dictates that men wear shirts and women wear blouses. Women can also wear shirts, but men can't wear blouses; a classic example of a nonsensical double standard. The custom may have been a purely arbitrary convention that everyone followed without understanding why. There may have been a reason once, but it no longer exists. How we got to this stage isn't as important as what we do now.

Must this situation persist? Not at all. Customs and the roles of men and women are in a constant state of flux. Not long ago, it was unacceptable for women to wear slacks or pants in the work place. Now women can wear any men's fashions. They wear suits with pants, vests and ties. A major department store ran a huge advertisement for silk shirts and silk underwear for men. How far is that from women's clothes? Today's customs will certainly be modified tomorrow.

Some clothing is designed to accommodate the physical differences between men and women. A man can wear a bra, and a woman can wear a jock; but those articles of clothing are most useful for members of a particular sex. Other articles of clothing are designed to accommodate ease of use in the bathroom. A man can wear panties, and a woman can wear boxer shorts; but those articles are more functional for members of a particular sex.

There have always been those who push the barriers of acceptable attire. Even motorcycle riders now have long hair and wear earrings. Who will tell the guy in black leather riding a Harley, that his long hair and stud earring make him a wimp? What about members of Royalty? They wear the fanciest, finest materials with lace, pleats and frills. Show-business performers go far beyond any standard dress code. Have you ever watched MTV and tried to identify the performer as a man or a woman? If you have enough money or notoriety, no one questions what you wear. More likely you're considered a trend setter. Finally, who would call a brawny Scot lad a sissy for wearing a kilt? And why isn't a kilt a skirt? And if it is a skirt, why is it okay for men to wear? Why are things this way? You guessed it, *currently accepted custom.*

If you want to wear women's clothing, why shouldn't you? Why shouldn't your ideal, open society (the one you're dreaming about) exist? Consider this —

— There is no legitimate justification for most clothing to be considered appropriate attire only for the members of a particular sex.
— Standards of appropriate attire change constantly.
— Recent trends have blurred the distinctions between the dressing habits of the sexes and have placed society on the path towards your shared vision.
— Therefore, you just have to keep pushing in that direction.

The Biblical Argument

Ooops. You knew there was a clinker, and it must be the Bible. There will be someone who uses the Bible in an attempt to prove that you are a pervert and fill you with guilt and shame. Do they have a point? There is *only one* Scripture that addresses the subject of cross-dressing —

> *"A woman must not wear men's clothing,*
> *and a man must not wear women's clothing . . ."*

> — Deuteronomy, Chapter 22, Verse 5

What does that mean? One of the most popular commentaries, *Commentary on the Whole Bible* by James M. Gray, doesn't even mention the verse. Apparently he didn't think it was that im-

portant. Doctor Gray cautions against concentrating on small portions of the Bible to draw conclusions. He encourages serious stu-
dents to study multiple chapters in order to obtain a comprehensive
knowledge and place individual verses in their proper perspective.
Many who quote the Bible could learn a great deal from that advice.
Other authors do comment but ascribe differing interpretations.

In *Manners and Customs of the Bible*, Reverend James M. Free-
man explains that pagan religions frequently worshipped idols de-
picting the features of one sex and the clothing of the opposite sex.
Worshippers often cross-dressed to participate in religious rituals.
So one interpretation is to avoid cross-dressing because it was part of
idol worship.

George M. Lamsa, the author of *Old Testament Light,* points
out that in the Eastern culture women were generally respected and
not searched or molested. They were allowed to travel relatively freely.
Men dressed as women might be able to smuggle contraband or spy
on their enemies. Are you a smuggler? A spy?

It is common knowledge that women were typically excluded
from religious ceremonies. A woman sometimes dressed like a man
in order to gain access to the worship service. This interpretation
has particular appeal because the verse is first directed at women
and then at men. In most verses the important point comes first followed by points of lesser importance.

What is the proper interpretation when even the religious experts disagree? Most fail to even mention transvestites. If it is wrong
for a man to wear a dress, then it is just as wrong for a woman to
wear a suit; yet few religious leaders comment when a woman wears
pants and a tie. Why don't they comment? The other 29 verses are
largely ignored, yet two seem curiously related. Verses 11 and 12
say, "Don't wear clothing woven from two kinds of thread: for in-
stance, wool and linen together. You must sew tassels on the four
corners of your cloaks."

One might ask why there isn't a great disturbance about the
blended fabrics commonly worn today by both men and women.
And how would the world react to tassels? How indeed. Other matters which the world pays little attention to, get far more emphasis in

the Bible. Why not focus on the more important ones? One can reasonably conclude that at best, there has been highly selective usage of Biblical phrases to support the attack on cross-dressers. More commonly, some individuals are intent on using the Bible to deceive others.

The Biblical argument is on shaky ground, and it simply isn't an issue. If someone insists on using a religious prohibition to attack you, refer them to this passage —

> *"... and forgive us our sins, just as we have forgiven those who have sinned against us ... Your heavenly father will forgive those who sin against you; but if you refuse to forgive them, he will not forgive you."*

> — Matthew, Chapter 6, Verses 12, 14 & 15

The book that your critics profess to follow states that God will treat them the way they treat others. Those who are intolerant are setting themselves up for serious consequences according to their own standards. The Bible is my source of spiritual nurture, and my intent is to stop others from using it to inappropriately criticize us. If your critics read the Bible with an open mind, they would find that Jesus never made anyone feel guilty. He welcomed those who were shunned by the sophisticated aristocracy. His followers were the poor, the prostitutes, the tax collectors, the fishermen; common, everyday people. He showed them love and respect. There was, however, one group that he continually criticized — the religious leaders. He referred to them as hypocrites because they acted holy while placing burdens on the people.

> *"Woe to you, Pharisees, and you religious leaders! You are like beautiful mausoleums — full of dead men's bones, and of foulness and corruption. You try to look like saintly men, but underneath those pious robes of yours are hearts besmirched with every sort of hypocrisy and sin."*

> — Matthew, Chapter 23, Verses 27-28

Where Does That Leave Us?

To dress in a certain manner as a matter of self-expression is fine. There is no rationale that you can't be your own person. Cross-dressing isn't for everybody; but if you want to, do it. If all fashions were equally acceptable for men and women, most people would probably dress much as they already do. There would be a group including most of us, who would wear clothing that spans the sexes.

When I started cross-dressing, I focused on women's undergarments. My lack of self-confidence was a strong contributing factor. I didn't like my looks. I didn't have good social skills. I had few dates. Still I had the same feelings as other men. Not having much success with women probably enhanced my interest in women's underwear. According to some therapists, portions of my background match a traditional profile of a cross-dresser. That may be true, but I have progressed beyond any fixation with sexy underwear, to thoroughly enjoy blouses, skirts, dresses and other accessories. I have a high consciousness of what I like and dislike in fashions. While I am working on a few unresolved issues, I am no longer stuck in undergarments, (although that's not a bad place to be stuck).

There is a point where cross-dressing indicates a problem. If you are using dressing as an escape mechanism, then that action is harmful to you. It's not the dressing that's harmful, it's *why* you are dressing. If you dress as an escape mechanism, seek competent, professional advice.

Is It Time for a Change?

If you keep pushing on the cross-dressing issue, you will find that there isn't any substance behind the prohibition. You have just accepted it and allowed it to rob you of your deserved happiness and enjoyment. Isn't it time to take a stand for what you believe? There are consequences in taking a stand, but there are also consequences in not taking a stand. Aren't the rewards worthwhile? What time do you think it is?

"There is a right time for everything:
A time to be born . . .
A time to plant . . .
A time to heal . . .
A time to rebuild . . .
A time to find . . .
A time for throwing away . . .
A time for repair . . .
A time to speak up . . .
A time for loving . . .
Everything is appropriate in its own time . . .
So I conclude that, first, there is nothing better
for a man than to be happy
and to enjoy himself as long as he can; and second,
that he should eat and drink
and enjoy the fruits of his labors,
for those are gifts from God."

— Ecclesiastes, Chapter 3, Selected Verses

There is a time for everything. It is time to understand and accept ourselves. It is time to heal ourselves. It is time to join the mainstream.

It is time for you to act!

Chapter 5

Understanding Sexuality

I have to live with myself, and so,
I want to be fit for myself to know;
I want to be able as days go by
Always to look myself straight in the eye;
I don't want to stand with the setting sun
And hate myself for the things I've done.
I don't want to keep on a closet shelf
A lot of secrets about myself,
And fool myself as I come and go
Into thinking that nobody else will know
The kind of a man I really am;
I don't want to dress myself up in sham.
I want to go out with my head erect,
I want to deserve all men's respect;
But here in the struggle for fame and pelf,
I want to be able to like myself.
I don't want to think as I come and go
That I'm bluster and bluff and empty show.
I never can hide myself from me,
I see what others may never see,
I know what others may never know,
I never can fool myself – and so,
Whatever happens, I want to be
Self-respecting and conscience free.

— Edgar Albert Guest

The Sexual Search

It was time to begin exploring who I was, and the most important question was my sexuality. I knew it was a major factor in my cross-dressing, but everything I'd ever heard about carried negative connotations. I didn't know the truth and was afraid to find out. Yet I knew that I must explore it. Fortunately my wonderful correspondents helped me. I had intentionally picked one who presented a strong, sexual image, and our interactions aided a great deal. However, I obtained the greatest insights from Tracy, who didn't project that image but became a close friend and openly discussed the question. With the hope of becoming healthy, I found the courage to explore what I thought and how I felt.

I learned a great deal about myself. What I learned was true for me, but my answers don't fit everyone. Instead, there is a unique set of answers for each one of us — the truth. Your answers will certainly differ from mine. Whatever conclusions you reach, the process of understanding your sexual identity is crucial. Be honest with yourself. If you lie to yourself, how can you accept yourself? If you don't accept yourself, how can anyone else accept you? If you aren't accepted by yourself and others, how can you ever be happy and satisfied? You may not like everything you find. You may begin changing parts of yourself. But to find peace and contentment, you must first understand and accept yourself as you are.

If this seems scary, welcome to the club. So far this has been mostly fun; a bit of a challenge, but generally easy. From here on it is work. However, doing the work will provide the greatest benefits. My first question was —

Am I a *Transsexual*[1]?

I started here because it seemed the most likely outcome. I enjoyed wearing women's clothing. I obtained strong, sexual gratifica-

---

[1]A person who believes that their true sexual identity is incongruous with their physical body. The male-to-female transsexual believes he is a woman trapped inside a man's body.

tion from wearing those clothes. I identified with the appearance of women. Therefore I must be a transsexual. How else could I explain this situation? The problem was that even though the concept was appealing, I didn't feel like a woman trapped inside a man's body. I am not a woman. I am not a little girl. I am not trapped in a man's body. I am a man. I enjoy being a man. Since that is all true, I could not be a transsexual. Yet I enjoy wearing women's clothing. What does this mean? What should I do now? I was confused and didn't know where to turn for clarification.

One question in the Boulton & Park survey started me thinking differently. It asked if I'd like to become a woman on demand and then return to being a man on demand. It was a provocative concept. I came to realize that I didn't want to be a woman. I wanted to temporarily take on the appearances of a woman. I also knew that society didn't approve of a man taking on such an appearance. The dichotomy of wanting to cross-dress while anticipating strong disapproval, placed me in a state of internal confusion. In my confused state, I had concluded that I must be a transsexual. Now I understood that it was my perception of what was acceptable that had caused me to consider myself a transsexual. That perception was wrong.

Perhaps we get trapped into thinking we are transsexuals partially as a result of the emphasis on *passing*[2]. As we try to pass, do we begin to believe that we are, or should be, women? Is the ability to pass a wonderful gift or a curse in disguise? Does it keep us from understanding the truth and coming out as our true selves?

Does the way we use female names contribute to the problem? We use the names to enhance our feminine impression, for security and for privacy. Sometimes we also use the names as part of an escape from reality. Do we confuse ourselves by over-using our female identity and thereby lose part of our male identity? When you see names in our publications, do you ever wonder if the person is a man or a woman? How can you tell for certain? If Robert, a male-to-female cross-dresser, adopts the name Roberta, and refers to himself

---

[2]The practice whereby a male creates an overall appearance that is designed to make him seem to be a woman.

as a she, what happens to Robert? Does he get lost as Robert becomes Roberta? Hiding behind these identities can make it difficult for ourselves and others to figure out who we are.

Similarly, we often speak of our *en femme* persona in the third person as if she is a separate person. She is not separate. She is an integral part of us. That manner of speaking perpetuates splitting our personality and adds to the confusion.

Consider the concept of *transitioning*[3]. It assumes that a man must live full-time as a woman. It forces a choice between being male or female and causes a man to abandon his maleness. Why should we free one aspect of ourselves only to imprison another? We haven't improved our overall condition by swapping one set of restrictions for another. This either/or concept takes us away from being ourselves and further confuses the situation.

There is also the phenomenon of *secondary transsexuals*[4]. Typically, these people did not experience the childhood feelings of being trapped in the wrong body. Instead, the condition usually developed later in life. Many of us come out of our self-imposed closets in our forties and fifties. Do we conclude that becoming a woman would be an answer to life's problems? Is this our version of a mid-life crisis? Are we meant to be women, or are we having trouble being men?

During my journey I learned several interesting things. Statistically, most people are heterosexual, but few are *completely* heterosexual. Everyone has a dominant sexual identity, but nearly all also possess one or more other sexual orientations to a degree. We tend to label someone 100% heterosexual when, in reality, they may be 98% heterosexual but experience occasional fantasies about a member of their same sex. Even our mixture of sexual feelings is subject to change over time. A man who considers himself a bisexual may prefer to have a sexual encounter with a woman at one time in his life and, later, prefer a man. Certain people think they belong in one

---

[3]The practice whereby a male seeks to live full time in a manner that is considered typical of a woman.
[4]A person who later in life believes that he or she is a transsexual.

category but actually belong in another. I started out thinking that I might be a transsexual, and that turned out to be incorrect.

At the core of these misconceptions is our failure to get in touch with our inner selves. We don't know enough about ourselves to assess our sexuality. At times I felt that I belonged in each of the sexual categories. It was shocking to find out that I didn't know much about that part of me. I had always considered myself to be reasonably intelligent and aware, but I was confused about this topic. Many of us become confused and burdened by inappropriate feelings of sexual guilt and shame. We need to break those chains.

An extra benefit I derived was a greater understanding and tolerance of others. I discovered that I held negative, stereotypical views about people with sexual orientations different from mine. When those feelings came to the surface, I felt foolish for having them. I needed an attitude adjustment and got one. I can't fully understand and relate to the members of other groups, since I haven't experienced the same feelings. But I have developed a higher degree of compassion for others and realize that, regardless of our sexual orientation, we are all equally important to the health of our community.

None of this was easy. I did a great deal of reading and corresponding. Some seek professional assistance. It won't happen over night, but it holds the key to self-understanding.

What do you think? Remember, you want the truth, not what others think. Whatever you decide is okay. Ask yourself —

Are you a transsexual?

Do you feel like a woman trapped inside a man's body?
Is it okay for you to be a transsexual? How about others?
Is society's negative view of cross-dressing a factor in seeing yourself as a woman?

Do you think you might be a secondary transsexual? Are you having difficulty coping with life?
Does the concept of transitioning confuse you?
Do you hide behind your feminine name, style and persona?
Are your feelings clear on this matter? Do you want professional help in sorting them out?
Are there other issues you need to consider about the question of transsexuality?
If you could adopt the appearances of a woman without ridicule, would you want to become a woman or would it be okay to remain a man?
Will passing as a woman solve your problems?

You may consider transsexuality a gender-identification issue rather than a sexual one. Regardless of the classification, it is a crucial question to be answered in determining your sexual identity. While it became clear that I wasn't a transsexual, that discovery didn't make the next question any easier —

Am I a *Homosexual* [5]?

Once again, the outcome was unclear. We brand any male who wears women's clothing as a homosexual. That outlook made me uncomfortable, and I didn't know how to deal with it. I decided to practice disregarding the stereotypes that I had listened to in the

---

[5] A person who has a definite preferential sexual attraction to persons of the same sex.

past. I was determined to discover how I felt, independent of what others said.

Even though I liked to wear women's clothing, I did not feel attracted to men. I was attracted to women. Dressing like a woman didn't mean I wanted to sleep with a man. Actually, the more I cross-dressed, the more I confirmed my attraction to women. If men truly didn't interest me, how could I be homosexual? I couldn't. Why was that so hard to find out? Why was I afraid of even asking the question? I had previously convinced myself that I wasn't afraid to ask. Of course I wasn't afraid, I just didn't have the time. I'll do it next week, or next month, soon. I finally stopped avoiding it. I faced my fears and found out they weren't terrible.

Once again I saw that my own good sense and clear thinking had become clouded. Society's prejudicial opinion of men who wear women's clothing and of homosexuals, had overridden my thoughts. I confess to having adopted prejudices in the past, but I overcame those society-induced fears by working with gays. One of the best businessmen I have ever worked for was gay. Several admired and respected co-workers were lesbians. I found them to be exactly like anyone else. They come in all sizes, shapes, colors and characteristics. Knowing people like them caused the stereotypes to disintegrate. It no longer mattered to me if someone was homosexual. Why should it?

Don't let potential difficulties deter you from self-examination. Without the truth, happiness will be elusive. What do you think? Whatever you decide is okay. So —

Are you a homosexual?

Are you sexually attracted by men? How about women?
Do you want to have a physically intimate relationship with another man? With a woman?
Is it possible to have such a relationship with a member of the same sex without being a homosexual?

| Is it okay for you to be a homosexual? How about others? |
| How do your emotions and feelings fit in this question? |
| Is homosexuality compatible with your current lifestyle? |
| Would you change anything in your life if you discovered you were a homosexual? |
| Do you need help understanding and accepting the truth? What support resources are available? Family? Friends? Correspondents? Therapists? |
| What should you do next? |

I was making progress but there were additional worrisome questions. I found myself fascinated by two of the male-to-female cross-dressers with whom I had corresponded. They had sent several photos that I found attractive and exciting. My reaction disturbed me and reinforced my fears. Once again society discouraged seeking the truth. It seemed easier, if not better, not to look at the question. Finally, I looked. When is this going to get easy? Next question —

Am I *Bisexual* [6]?

Each revelation had lead to another difficult question. Now I found myself thinking that I might be bisexual. How else could I explain this situation? The pictures had turned me on. They were guys. Didn't that make me bisexual? After a while it became apparent that it was their appearance as women that attracted me. While I

---

[6]A person who has approximately equal sexual attraction to persons of the same sex as to those of the opposite sex.

was attracted by the impression, I finally understood that I wasn't attracted by a man. An early draft of this section precipitated an intense conversation with my wife. She interpreted my comments as indicating a lustful, sexual outlook of women. In reality, I was projecting their feminine appearance onto myself. I wanted to adopt the sexy, feminine image that I saw in others, whether women or men dressed as women. I am moving to more conservative fashions, but these long-denied feelings needed expression, and my wife understands that need.

It took a while to acknowledge my feelings. Then, while admitting the attraction, I realized that I was free to choose not to act on those feelings. I could have erotic feelings for women and for the feminine mystique displayed by cross-dressers without being bad. I could admit my true feelings while reaffirming my commitment to my marriage. It was not an either/or choice. I could stop denying the truth. What a liberating discovery.

I was beginning to feel remarkably better. Finding answers to difficult questions was infinitely better than remaining in the dark. I had suffered far too much for far too long. I could see all of the problems caused by believing the negative stereotypes. I could see how those negative thoughts repressed my true spirit, how they caused me to be far less happy and content than I could be. It was definitely time for a change.

Okay, it's your turn again. Remember, it's the truth that counts. Well, —

Are you bisexual?

Do you have sexual feelings toward both men and women?
Do you only have those feelings toward men who are dressed as women?
Must you act on or explore these feelings?

Could your feelings be of warmth and compassion rather than purely sexual?
What is your attraction to multi-sex relationships? Having an affair? Group sex?
Is it okay for you to be bisexual? How about others?
Does having erotic sexual feelings make you a bad person?
Are you concerned about your feelings or the reaction of society?
What do you want to do about this question?

Where Am I Now?

Where did that leave me? Am I a transsexual? No. Am I a homo-sexual? No. Am I bisexual? No. Well, what then? The only choice that society seemed to have left was sexual deviant. Maybe they were right after all. I had never seen any indication that men who felt and acted as I did, could possibly be normal, well-adjusted, functional or productive people. They were always pictured as warped. How do I live with that?

Thank God for my correspondents, *Tapestry* and Virginia Prince's books. By myself I felt lost and unable to cope. With these resources I had found enough positives to know that I wasn't alone. I found well-educated, bright, considerate, spiritual, family-oriented men who shared similar feelings. There were so many of us who were solid citizens by any reasonable definition, that it was incomprehensible that we could all be perverts. There had to be another answer, but what?

Am I *Sexy?*

Could sex be one of the common threads? Many men are turned

on by a woman wearing sexy undergarments. If men perceive some-thing as sexy on a woman, why couldn't they see it as sexy on themselves? It seems reasonable to me.

I grew up with a complete supply of sexual hang-ups. Didn't we all? Those hang-ups inhibited the fun my wife and I could have together. When I finally divulged my cross-dressing desires to her, we began to explore ways that both of us could wear sexy lingerie. The result? I don't have to sneak around to try to wear sexy clothes. Wearing lingerie became a release for my sexual inhibitions and pro-vided a harmless even desirable avenue for long-suppressed exhibi-tionism. From all of this analysis I concluded that I was basically a heterosexual male with repressed sexuality who wished to explore becoming all that he could. That sounded healthy.

Is wanting to be sexy exclusively for women? Is dressing and acting sexy unhealthy for men? Is there only one formula to follow for dressing and behaving? I used to try to deny my sexuality; now I'm finding out what it is. Why do other people make such a big deal out of this? Are they afraid of having the same feelings themselves?

How would you feel if there were no sexual constraints? Re-member, the sky is the limit, and whatever you decide is okay, —

Are you sexy?

Are you a sexy person? Do you want to be sexy? Is there any-thing wrong with that?
Can you be sexy and remain a man rather than becoming a woman?
Are you simply a normal, healthy male?
Why shouldn't you wear clothes that give you pleasure?
Are sex and clothing the same thing? How are they connected for you?

In what ways would you like to express your sexuality? Where, when and how can you do that without causing problems for others?
Do you have to be sexy all the time?
Does having erotic sexual feelings make you a bad person?

How Did It Turn Out?

How did your self-examination process come out? Whatever results you found are okay. The important thing is knowing the truth. Whether bisexual, heterosexual, homosexual, transsexual or a mixture, we are all human beings. Why worry about sub-groups and categories? Now that you understand yourself better, invest more energy in accepting yourself as you are. Incorporate the truth of what you found into your life. It may be extremely difficult. It may take time. It may cause upsets, but consider the benefits. Find a resolution that benefits you and those you love. If you have serious issues, seek professional assistance. You and I are not qualified to deal with deep sexual and emotional problems alone. There are many who can help. There is no reason to continue to suffer in silence. Get Help!

You have updated the picture with the beginning of your foundation, understanding sexuality. That foundation will lift you above the current reality and closer to the shared vision and your personal style. Congratulations on a giant step. Don't worry if you can't resolve this question in a short period of concentrated effort. It takes a long time. I took six months. The important thing is to work until you discover the truth. Take all the time you need, and pledge to yourself that you will —

Shared Vision – An Open Society

Your Personal Style

Understanding Sexuality

Current Reality – A Closed Society

Find the truth!

Understanding Emotions

"It's great that men bang drums and bond in the woods, that they're getting together to redefine their sense of male identity, but in order to be whole, in order to be loved and loving, in order to have relationships 'with women,' men also need to gain possession of their feminine identity, and this cannot be accomplished in isolation from women. For while drumming and bonding define a man as a man – in terms of his strength, his tribe, his father . . . being in possession of his female essence gives him community, brings his heart home. And coming home to the feminine is what we all need to do now."

— Daphne Rose Kingma
The Men We Never Knew

It Is Not About Dressing as a Woman

Just a minute there bucko. Everyone knows that dressing in women's clothing is the issue. Where do you get off telling me it isn't. I was willing to look at difficult things in a different way. I even let you turn me inside-out exploring sexuality. But this is stretching too far. It can't be true. Are you sure it isn't true? Before you label me kooky, take a close look. This is deeper than clothes. It is about bringing all of the separate components of ourselves together so we can become — *A Whole Person*.

Cross-dressing gets the attention, but isn't the core issue. In our letters, magazines and books, plenty is said about the duality or polarization of our nature; the separation of feminine gender traits from the male sex. We talk as though two distinct people inhabit our bodies and that we must let that 'little girl' locked inside of us get out. If we dress-up, make up and act like women, everything will be fine. This concept of duality gets us into trouble. We aren't two separate people. *We are one.* We have become fragmented by compartmentalizing ourselves. One compartment is a man and exhibits traditional masculine traits. The other compartment strives to become a woman and exhibits traditional feminine traits. We learned previously that customs have dictated appropriate clothing for men and women, but they also have dictated character traits. Through this practice our culture has created a firm, but arbitrary, link between sex and gender. While that link has caused enormous problems, it also supplies a powerful unifying force because — *Our greatest common bond is that each of us in our own way is trying to bend, shift, stretch or break, that culturally enforced link between sex and gender.*

We add to the confusion and diffuse our energy by using alternate terminology and by attaching different meanings to the same words. I was encouraged to find that we are actually quite close in our thinking, and it's usually just the words that get in the way. Terms and concepts such as *androgyny, alternative gender expression, the third sex* and *transgendered people*, share a common theme. They promote finding ways to create our own unique blend of traits and characteristics to become whole. Our job is to support each other's right of self-expression.

This picture contrasts the

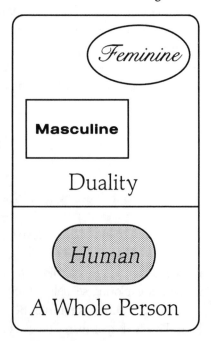

separation and incompleteness inherent in the philosophy of duality, with the rich fullness of becoming a whole person. It shows our masculine and feminine gender traits merging to form the person we were meant to be, the real us. Striving for that joy of wholeness continues to motivate me to make difficult changes. That motivation is highly contagious.

What Is a Man?

How do we define what it means to be a man? The key elements of the macho-male syndrome are —

Anti-femininity — Manhood means never doing anything that even remotely suggests femininity. That's sissy stuff, stuff for girls. We must relentlessly repudiate and devalue anything feminine for ourselves. Allowing it to become part of us makes us less of a man.

Success — Manhood is measured by power, wealth and success. Competition is a general philosophy of life. The winner is the one who dies with the most toys, and we must win.

Aggressiveness — Manhood means exuding an aura of daring and aggression. Go for it. Show no softness or sympathy. Don't let anyone or anything stand in the way. Crush any obstacle.

Self-reliance — Manhood means never asking for help. Be reserved emotionally. Be cool, unflappable, tough, in control. Be dependable in a crisis. We must never, under any circumstances, reveal our true feelings.

Sound familiar? We've all seen countless versions but guess what? That behavior model has made emotional wrecks of us. It has caused untold damage to those around us as we crush everyone and everything we touch. We will suffer nearly any consequence, but, no matter what, we are not going to be like a woman. That behavior borders on terminal stupidity.

I am a man. Society says men should be strong. I have feelings. Society says feelings reveal softness and softness is only for women. How can I be a man and have feelings? Our culture pressures me to create two separate persons. I act outwardly as a man. When I want to express my feelings, I adopt my female persona. If I don't keep them separate, society shows disapproval. No wonder I've separated myself. Do I want to separate myself? No. Is it best for me? No. They say that if I show my feelings, others will surely take advantage of me. So I must protect myself and never let anyone see how I feel. Isn't it strange that, no matter how badly it hurts me, I still cling to that perverted, macho-male syndrome that lacks any semblance of balance?

Integration And Balance

We have labeled clothing and behavior as either masculine or feminine even though, in the majority of cases, they are neither. We like things to be black or white and try to make everything an either/or choice. But the world isn't black and white. It is an infinite variety of shades of gray, a continuous line rather than two extreme points. One can occupy any point on the continuum. He can exhibit parts of "A" and parts of "B" to varying degrees. He moves closer to one of the end points as his balance point changes. The key is balance, not choosing "one or the other."

We can create greater balance in our lives by integrating the dual aspects of our nature. We are part male and female, part active and passive, part dominant and submissive, part "A" and "B". All of these parts contribute to the total, and we will be healthier when we stop denying or judging parts and accept all of them. Therapists advise that striving for wholeness is the healthiest path to reaching our potential. A fundamental principle of Eastern religions and philosophies stresses oneness and balance since the way we think, what we believe and how we act determines our health. How healthy can it be to separate ourselves into male and female compartments? How healthy can it be to only enter the female compartment secretly?

Can only women be appreciative, caring, compassionate, considerate, gentle, gracious, sensitive, soft, sympathetic? Rather than defining the difference between men and women, these qualities should simply be considered human. Perhaps the male of the species, while wielding power and control, isn't such a healthy human after all. Maybe men should be more like women; better integrated and better balanced.

My Journey

I felt good about the results of my exploration of sexuality, and my work shifted to another difficult question, Who am I emotionally? Who is inside under the facade that I show to the world? Is my true self so hidden that even I wouldn't recognize him?

My journey to find myself began in earnest almost 15 years ago as I approached that magical age of 40. I had always repressed my true feelings, but, then, I began to examine my feelings about work, spirituality and emotions. I began to understand and accept myself as I was and became more comfortable with my ideas. I began to pour out my pent-up anxieties and release what I had previously kept guarded deep inside. It was the first time I had ever allowed myself to get in touch with my inner self.

I stopped pretending to be macho by hiding all my doubts and fears. Gradually I came to understand that I had feelings of softness, tenderness and compassion . . . and that was okay. I felt doubts and fears . . . and that was okay. I cried . . . and that was okay. I hugged another man . . . and that was okay. Having these feelings didn't stop me from being a man, they actually made me more human. Showing these feelings was healthy, whereas holding them inside made me unhappy. I began to find out who I was, deep down inside. The more I explored, the more I liked myself.

I am learning to integrate all of my parts and become whole. I finally let myself enjoy decorating our new home with my wife. Everyone knows that a real man doesn't enjoy decorating. Well I did, and we had a great time decorating together. Now it's truly *our* house. I show my feelings more with friends and family. Amazingly, many of them respond in a positive manner. It feels good. I am finally acknowledging my appreciation for art, music, color, clothing, fabrics and textures. Rather than the world collapsing around my ears, it is expanding and becoming more fulfilling. Life is much richer. In the past I denied myself pleasures. I thought someone might disapprove. I was the loser. Now I'm doing these things and feeling better about myself. I've also discovered that I'm not a cross-dresser or a transvestite. *What?* Don't be surprised by that statement. I can say it inasmuch as those terms are too limiting. Besides, I am not a *what*, I am a *who*, and a complicated who at that. Who am I?

I am a person

I am a person who has strong spiritual beliefs.
I am a person who loves his wife and is committed to his marriage.
I am a person who values his family and friends.
I am a person who knows that being a grandfather
is one of the greatest experiences of life.
I am a person who delights in children and childlike things.
I am a person who is sensitive, caring and compassionate.
I am a person who believes in personal responsibility.
I am a person who is committed to working hard
and doing a good job.
I am a person who enjoys good food and fine wines
(plus beer, pizza and ice cream).
I am a person who brings humor to the workplace and elsewhere.
I am a person who works at physical conditioning
and enjoys long distance running.
I am a person who is fond of animals, especially cats.
I am a person who is discovering
an appreciation of theater and the arts.
I am a person who is learning to express his enjoyment
of decorating, color, fabrics and textures.
I am a person who enjoys wearing clothing
that society views as feminine.

That is a great deal more than simply being called a transvestite or cross-dresser. I am a person, a very complex person.

Connect With the Feminine

My desire to cross-dress and act out a feminine role had become clear, but Ms. Kingma's book opened my eyes even wider. She is a psychotherapist with significant experience working with men who have difficulty handling emotions. Her work confirms that women desire an intimate relationship with men; that women often feel they haven't been getting that type of relationship; and that they have been berating men for their insensitivity and failure to provide the desired relationship. Rather than continuing this mutually destructive path, she says we need to understand that —

- Men do have feelings,
- They have been victimized by society's insistence on hiding those feelings, and
- Women can build bridges to their desired intimate relationships by making it safe for their man to explore and express his feelings.

Think about that. Women want intimate relationships with men. That intimacy requires men to be in touch with their feelings. Most men have difficulty dealing with their feelings. Who would argue with that? There is a higher level of sensitivity, compassion, feeling and caring in our community compared to the general male population. We don't have as many macho-male bulldozers. What does that mean? It means that, in general, we are more in touch with our emotions and feelings. That also means that we are closer to being able to provide the intimate relationships women want. That is great news, because we can be the vanguard of a significant social improvement.

What if . . .

we understood that integrating our softer side into our lives was what women want from us? Would we have a more positive view of ourselves?

What if . . .

women understood that the underlying softness that led us into dressing and acting differently is also a key to achieving intimacy? Would they have a more positive and supportive view of us?

What if . . .

each of us created an intimate relationship with our spouse or significant other? Would that be the beginning of changing society's perception of us?

What if . . .

we integrated the male propensity to act and the female propensity to feel? Would that form the basis of a new standard for being human?

Face the Devil

We can make those "What ifs" come true by modifying our behavior. Sometimes we choose not to acknowledge certain aspects of ourselves because we don't like or are uncomfortable with them. We are unwilling to open the closet doors and look inside. We don't know what devils are lurking in the dark. The devils are there, so denial won't make them go away. The way to free ourselves from them is to open the door, turn on the light and look at them. Instead of looking at them in fear and judgment, choose to look at them through the eyes of love and acceptance.

> *"Don't deny your past, embrace it, grow from it.*
> *Denial is the destroyer of spirit and soul.*
> *(Denial is the devil. Without denial, there is no sin.)"*

> — Heather Hatfield
> "Denial is the Devil"

Some people point out our shortcomings and tell us how we don't quite fit the acceptable mold. They try to get us to deny who we are by making us believe that we are not good enough. That is a lie, and the lie drags us down. The problem is not who we are. The problem is denying who we are. When we face the truth, we find that we are better than we thought and often start to fix the things we don't like so much. By facing the truth, we actually get better.

"Wouldn't it be great if I could be my real self with myself? With my friends, my lovers, my parents? Myself with my brothers and sisters, at my job. Spontaneous - that's the word, that's the feeling I want. Unconstricted. Uninhibited, in a safe and loving way. Just as wild, as crazy, as happy, as scared, as moved as I feel about other things in my life. Vulnerable. Honest. Engaged and alive. Down with the walls, the defenses, the games, the lies, the bravado."

—Greg Schwartz
Straightjacket

A major indication of success in our adventure will be when legions of us start tearing down the walls we hide behind and begin letting the world see us as we are. Some of us have wished to wake up in the body of a woman — then we could be happy. Not likely. Instead, we need to accept ourselves as we are.

What About You?

If you shed all the imposed male images, preconceived notions, impossible dreams and facades, who would you be? Forget who you think you should be. Forget who society says you should be. Look inside and get to know and understand yourself better. You have great hidden treasures that you never let anyone, including yourself, see. Why continue to pretend? Who are you pretending for? Don't be blinded by your fantasies, just recognize them. Don't judge what you think or feel as good or bad, just find out the truth. What do you think? Who are you emotionally? How do you feel? In the uniqueness that can only be you, —

Who are you?

What adjectives would you use to describe yourself?
What do you enjoy doing?
How would you describe your emotions and feelings?
What are your inner needs?
What is your personal vision of life?
How does your view of gender fit your lifestyle?
What kinds of relationships do you want?
What are your motivations?
What do you want to achieve with your life? What is most important to you?
What keeps you from being what you want to be?
Are you inhibited by society? By your own fantasies? By a lack of confidence?
What can you do to overcome the barriers that hold you back? What steps can you take to make your life better?

You've finished your foundation with understanding emotions, and that is the most difficult task in this process. What remains is far from easy, but you have a solid base to build on. Beginning to develop a true picture of who you are, has opened wide vistas for the future. Your dreams can become reality. Reaching them is within your power. The message is unchanged; work until you discover the truth about your emotions. Take all the time you need and renew your pledge to yourself to —

Shared Vision – An Open Society

Your Personal Style

Understanding Emotions

Understanding Sexuality

Current Reality – A Closed Society

Find the truth!

We Can Make Changes

"I have often heard cross-dressers say society will not accept us, or the public isn't ready for us, or some similar statement. Of course it's true, and the public will never be accepting of us until we are accepting of ourselves and are accepting of society. The world will never invite us out into it in our clothing/gender choice. The only way the world will ever get used to seeing genetic males in a feminine gender form is by seeing us and interacting with us."

— Janyne Cresap
"Going Public"

Can We Change Things?

Don't waste time looking for a shortcut to full acceptance by society. Consider what Janyne said. We have a difficult road ahead and must take all of the steps. First, we accept ourselves; then, we accept society; and, finally, society accepts us. Conventional wisdom advises us to give up and return to our closets. Society tells us to accept the current reality because it can't be changed. That's what they would like us to believe, but the opposite is true. Remember when —

— all blacks were slaves?
— factory workers owed their soul to the company store?
— women couldn't vote?
— gays and lesbians were totally in the closet?
— No Smoking sections didn't exist in restaurants?
— family planning clinics weren't even a gleam in someone's eye?
— all members of Congress were men?

Look back through the years and see how many major innovations have occurred in your lifetime. Conditions have always changed and are changing at an ever increasing rate. The question is not, "Will conditions change?" Rather, it is, "How will they change?"

Every significant transformation of the fabric of society has been led by a relatively small group of individuals who had a vision of something that didn't exist. They used various tactics to influence society in a way that was compatible with their vision. Most people took no action and simply went along for the ride. Your choice is to either work to influence society or do nothing but go along for the ride. If you like the way things are, don't do anything. But if you don't like the way things are, quit complaining and commit to achieving your vision. When you make that commitment, you can begin to transform society. It may not happen in the manner you expect or when you expect, but it will happen.

What's Possible?

Some people remember Jimmy Valvano as the hero who fought cancer. Others remember him as a man who lost his job over a point-shaving scandal. I remember him as the basketball coach whose team accomplished the impossible. The 1983 North Carolina State Wolfpack was a good basketball team, but most people didn't expect them to get into the NCAA tournament. They got in. Even fewer people expected them to win a game in the tournament. They won several games. The experts agreed that NC State could not get to the final four. They got to the final four. Everyone knew they couldn't win the tournament. Their chance of winning was compared to the likelihood of an elephant driving in the Indianapolis 500. Houston's *Phi Slamma Jamma* were prohibitive favorites. Everyone knew that Houston couldn't be beaten. Everyone was wrong. NC State did the impossible. They won the tournament. They had a vision and worked hard to achieve it.

Who decides what's possible and impossible? We mostly do that ourselves. Often we listen to conventional wisdom and convince ourselves that there is nothing we can do. So we do nothing, and nothing happens. We don't have to repeat that process. If enough of us share the vision of an open, accepting society, we will forever alter the fabric of society. The experts will not give us a chance, but they've been wrong before. We too can accomplish a miracle.

The inside story is that even the most powerful institutions are composed of people who are every bit as human as we are. They want us to believe that they are in total control, that their position is unassailable. The truth is, they are as susceptible to doubts and fears as the rest of us. This condition of reassuring anarchy tells us that even deeply rooted customs are more vulnerable than the experts and authorities want us to know.

Only your reluctance to get involved can hold you back. Begin the trip to achieve your vision and personal style by —

Making changes!

How?

"Behold the turtle.
He makes progress only when he sticks his neck out."

— James B. Conant

The Golden Rule

To be accepted as you are. To be free to dress and act out your desires. To be left in peace as long as you don't hurt anyone. Isn't that what you want? Life will be much better then. You aren't out to convert the world to your view, you just want to be accepted. How can you do it? By using the Golden Rule and treating others the way you want to be treated. It's simple, straightforward, and it works.

It places the burden on us to initiate positive actions, regardless of how we've been treated. It requires us to treat others well, even if the other person is treating us poorly. If we wait for society to treat us well, nothing will happen. Waiting for them could create a situation like the old Pennsylvania railroad law. It said that if two trains approach on intersecting tracks, both shall stop and neither shall proceed until the track is clear. I can envision two trains that reached an intersection in 1886 and, since neither can move until the track is clear, are both still waiting for the other train to make the first move. Someone must move first. It won't be of any value for us to be like a train waiting for society to take action. In order to be accepted, we must first accept others as they are, even if we don't agree with them.

It Is Us

There was a discussion on a radio talk show about the divisiveness of society. How we often set up a zero-sum game where whatever one side wins the other side loses. That approach always pits us against them. They made the point that as soon as we start looking at our differences, we move away from any sort of win/win solution. Each side justifies its position and makes the other's position unacceptable. Their conclusion was that we must stop that sort of divisive behavior. After all, when all of the battles are over there can be no more "them versus us" because there's no one left.

We won't always agree, but, to succeed, we must respect each other and each other's position. Without love and compassion for each other, we will find that Pogo was right, "We have met the enemy, and he is us." We must quit bickering over words, style, recognition and leadership and begin to fix ourselves.

There is great benefit for all of us in the process of acceptance. Even though we benefit, the act of acceptance is not being practiced with the goal of self-interest. It's not a matter of getting what I want. It's everyone getting what he or she wants. *It's us.*

Some people try to appear to be interested in others. They are only interested in themselves but put on the appearance of caring. They try to fool others into giving them what they want. That approach is fatally flawed for any lasting change. We can't *appear* to be interested in others; we have to be interested in others.

A few people subscribe to the personal interest rule, "Do unto them before they do unto me." They will try to take advantage of our generosity, and we must guard against that happening. But we cannot focus solely on taking care of ourselves, or no positive change will ever be made. Conditions will get progressively worse, and we will be ruled by the laws of the jungle. Most of us are not lions and tigers, and we won't be big winners in a jungle.

Rather than starting another cause, demanding our rights and continuing the hyphenation of America into pro-this or anti-that, let's use our energy to pull everyone together on the unifying principles of common interest and mutual benefit. It doesn't have to be either/or. It can be win/win.

We need to make a lasting commitment to change. We will be down many times but must get back up again. When Yoda was training Luke Skywalker to become a Jedi Warrior, Luke kept saying he would *try* to do it. Yoda's response was, "Not try, do." This is not another New Year's resolution to try for a few months. This is a New Life's resolution to do for a lifetime.

An Interesting Parallel

Much has been written about the plight of the black community. They feel the impact of discrimination and often despair because there is no lasting solution in sight. Their condition is a close parallel to the situation in the gender community. A number of black leaders advocate collective action against society to force advancement. But there is a growing number of black leaders who advocate individual effort within the American mainstream. Shouldn't we rely on individual effort? Shouldn't we join the mainstream rather than complaining and attacking from the outside?

Those same leaders advocate creating a collective identity to encourage diversity within the race. They seek an end of repression based on race. They see personal development as the highest challenge of the black community. Shouldn't we establish a collective identity and encourage diversity? Shouldn't we seek an end of repression based on gender or sexual stereotypes? Shouldn't we make personal development our highest challenge?

In discussing this collective identity, progressive black leaders often draw on their experiences. They admit that beneath surface acceptance there remains a pool of residual racism. They acknowledge the reality of racism but point out the enormous range of opportunities open to blacks. They urge blacks to use their initiative to take advantage of these opportunities to create a new society where they can enjoy equal membership. Shouldn't we learn from our experiences? While admitting the existence of prejudice, shouldn't we acknowledge the enormous opportunities open to us? Shouldn't we use our initiative to take advantage of these opportunities to create a new society where we can enjoy equal membership? Shouldn't we do these things?

Where Do We Start?

There is no better place to start using the Golden Rule than within our own gender community. Consider the dialog in our literature as one group puts down another. Some don't accept those who dress or act differently. Some don't accept those who dress in a sexually explicit fashion. Some cross-dressers don't accept homosexuals. Some transsexuals don't accept transvestites. Some organizations don't accept members with different views. Some leaders of organizations don't accept the leaders of other organizations. Far too often, we treat each other as badly as society treats us.

This prejudicial behavior isn't true of everyone in the gender community, but it is far too prevalent to ignore. How can we expect the rest of society to treat us well? All they have to do to justify rejecting us is to follow our own provincial actions. If we are intolerant of those who don't meet our expectations, how can we possibly hope that mainstream society will be tolerant of us? We certainly don't meet their expectations.

The strangest thing is that we have so much in common, yet we tend to focus on those aspects that differentiate the other person from ourselves. Why do we do that to each other? We all belong to the gender community. That fact alone should be enough to unite us. However our common bonds run far deeper. We live in the same political system and enjoy the same religious freedom. We enjoy the same fast foods, sitcoms and bad jokes. We live and work in the same marketplace. We share the same dreams, aspirations, doubts and fears for ourselves and for our children. With all those things in common, how can our differences be so overwhelming?

We have an immediate problem — to fix our own behavior. Most people want to fix a problem this afternoon so everything will be wonderful by dinner time. We want all solutions to be quick like a rabbit. I would love to say that we could do it quickly, but our rate of progress is likely to be slow and steady like a turtle. Everyone would like a quick fix. They certainly are quick, but they rarely are fixes. Lasting change takes time.

While you'd like to fix the world, there is an enormous amount of work to do on ourselves. The challenge is to begin treating others as you want to be treated. Let the change start with you. Accept others as they are, not as you think they should be. Give everybody the same chance you want to be given. Start with the idea that it is your turn. If you act in a reasonable, responsible manner, what you say and do to others will make a difference. You can help create a real gender community where we transcend our individual differences and demonstrate our interdependence.

You have accepted the shared vision of a society that is open and accepting of the gender community as a whole, as well as your own unique style. You have laid down a solid foundation by understanding your sexuality and emotions. Now, you've added the method, the Golden Rule, to achieve your goals. You also know where to start using it — right here in your own gender community. You are well on the path to success. All you have to do to make progress is to —

Shared Vision – An Open Society

Your Personal Style

Golden Rule

Understanding Emotions

Understanding Sexuality

Current Reality – A Closed Society

Stick your neck out!

Acceptance

> *"The supreme happiness of life*
> *is the conviction of being loved for yourself,*
> *or, more correctly,*
> *being loved in spite of yourself."*
>
> — Victor Hugo

First Step

You have already completed the hardest work by creating a vision, and now you can begin collecting more of the benefits. There are four key steps that will help complete the process of becoming whole and transforming society's attitudes. Acceptance is the first of those steps. Simply put, self-acceptance means to approve of yourself exactly as you are. With all of your quirks and shortcomings, you are okay. You aren't perfect, but you don't have to justify your imperfections. You don't have to pledge to fix them. You just have to acknowledge them. Self-acceptance is a key aspect of mental health, and it starts by thinking positively about yourself. What can you do to accept yourself better? Put the emphasis on *you*.

- Become *your* best friend
- Pay attention to *your* thoughts and feelings
- Trust *yourself* enough to act on what *you* think is right and makes *you* feel happy
- Respect *yourself*
- Be proud of who *you* are rather than trying to be like someone else
- Explore and appreciate *your* own special talents
- Learn from *your* failures rather than overreacting to them
- Learn to love *yourself* as a unique individual

Happiness is...

Accepting yourself today; being happy now, with the full knowledge that you have shortcomings; seeing yourself as having many aspects and characteristics. There are signs everywhere with slogans about what happiness is. Happiness is *(fill in the blank)*. Those signs and slogans are fine, but the slogan you ought to promote is: *True happiness is; accepting myself as I am.*

Learning to accept myself continues to be the most difficult task I have ever undertaken. I haven't found a shortcut or quick fix. I haven't found anyone who could do it for me. Working through this process has improved my life in ways I never imagined. I started by being true to myself. That was difficult because I was afraid that I might not like what I would find. However, I was hurting badly enough to start. As I faced the parts of me that I didn't like so much, they began to change. I just had to stop pretending. I wish that I had started sooner.

> *"Isn't it all right to say to them, 'I am so sorry I cannot be a banana. I would love to be a banana if I could for you, but I'm a peach.' And you know what? If you wait long enough, you'll find a peach lover. And then you can live your life as a peach, and you don't have to live your life as a banana. All the lost energy it takes to be a banana, when you're a peach."*

> — Leo Buscaglia
> *Living, Loving, & Learning*

Many of us are beautiful, luscious, peaches trying desperately to live up to society's view of a banana. Think of how healthy the world will be after each person has accepted themselves rather than trying to be someone else. Become the peach you were designed to be.

Take Control Of Your Life

A major thrust of this book is to encourage you to take control of your life and stop living as others expect you to. Find out who you are and let that spirit free. You have tremendous gifts locked inside which can benefit you and the world. Most hold back for one reason or another. Transvestism seems a good reason to hold back. It is your private devil, but *everyone* has a private devil. When you learn to accept your devil along with your neighbors' devils, everyone can quit playing spirit-crushing games and start being themselves.

You'll like the real you when you let that person out, so give yourself a chance to know you. You might be surprised how positively others react to the real you, so give them a chance to know you. Isn't it time to add the self-acceptance block to your picture and move closer to your goals? You do know that —

Shared Vision – An Open Society

Your Personal Style

Acceptance

Golden Rule

Understanding Emotions

Understanding Sexuality

Current Reality – A Closed Society

You are okay, just the way you are!

Share

"A friend is one to whom one may pour out
all the contents of one's heart,
chaff and grain together,
knowing that the gentlest of hands
will take and sift it,
keep what is worth keeping,
and with the breath of kindness,
blow the rest away."

— Arabian Proverb

My Journey

Several years ago I admitted my cross-dressing desires to my wife. She was surprisingly supportive. She encouraged me to dress in her presence several times. Those private sessions went fairly well, but a public appearance ended in laughter and heckling from those we met. I was emotionally unprepared to deal with that reaction, returned the entire issue to the closet and purged my clothes. I was afraid to face it. My wife had no desire to discuss the subject; consequently, I buried it for several years. I tried to hide from it, but we know the truth — the desire to cross-dress didn't go away.

This time was considerably different. As I corresponded with others who had similar feelings, I began to understand that I wasn't a bad person. I felt better. I no longer viewed cross-dressing as a dreadful secret to guard. I didn't have to hide from it any more. Although I wasn't ready for a public appearance, I knew that, in time, I would do better.

Our marriage has been built on trust and open communication. I intensely dislike hypocrisy, yet, out of fear of the response, found myself withholding a significant portion of myself from the person I loved most. That situation could not be allowed to continue if our marriage was to be rich and fulfilling. It became obvious that I had to reveal what was happening. This time I had to find a better way. We were taking a major vacation in about four months. I was determined that nothing would spoil it and decided to inform her after the trip. However, during a casual conversation, the speech that I had been planning came tumbling out. This unrehearsed event turned out to be the right time, place and manner for us.

Even though we have a strong bond, working through the issues remains difficult. We have both struggled. Our marriage is so important that I am willing to expend any amount of effort to protect it. Due to my commitment to remain a husband and maintain our existing lifestyle, my wife's fears were greatly alleviated.

We gradually reached the point where my wife agreed that I could dress at home. The main condition was that I remain a man. She didn't want her husband to be replaced by a girl friend. That was a reasonable bargain. First I began wearing sexy lingerie to bed. Then we had dinner at home with me totally *en femme*. Eventually we each wore lacy negligees, reclining on satin sheets in front of the fireplace. There was considerable gratification in these developments. My wardrobe moved out of its secret hiding place and into the closet alongside hers. That was a big moment. We even began to share clothing and jewelry. I could dress when we were home alone. There was no need to sneak opportunities. As a result, the intensity diminished. What a relief. I became freer to be me. It was an incredible personal growth experience. My hypocrisy vanished.

By nature, humans are usually in a hurry to get results. In the case of transvestism, moving too quickly can cause irreversible problems. My wife and I decided to live as though we had unlimited time available. That approach is working for us. Instead of worrying about the lost opportunities of the past, I look forward to many years of exploring my personal style, little by little. We did ourselves a big favor by giving ourselves enough time. It reduced the desire to rush in where angels should fear to tread.

That's my story, actually, our story. It isn't over, but we are on the right path. It is intense at times. It is often arduous. Sometimes it seems easier to stop talking, but how would things improve? They wouldn't, hence we persist. It will never end. We continue to rely on our love, friendship and open communication. It works.

It's All In How You Say It

Telling my wife turned out favorably, but the process is not without risk. Successfully sharing important news requires a strong commitment to each other. If the relationship is in trouble, the revelation of transvestism provides a convenient excuse to break it. One of my faithful correspondents repeatedly warned me that I should never tell my wife. He expressed great concern about what would happen, and, the fact is, exposing transvestite feelings has destroyed numerous relationships. Caution and thoughtful action is imperative.

I felt compelled to understand and accept myself before unveiling my feelings. Until then, I was too uncertain of myself to proceed. I had to know who I was and how I felt, before I could consider sharing my desires and vision. Once I became comfortable with my feelings, my focus shifted to looking for the right time, place and manner to inform my wife. I certainly didn't want to be discovered while I was cross-dressed. That situation is nearly impossible to explain. Assuming you have a strong relationship, sharing can work for you. You still have to understand and accept yourself. You still have to look for the right time, place and message. Those tasks are not easy. It took a year before I was ready to talk to my wife.

Other Views

This eloquent statement is from a cross-dresser, describing how
to disclose transvestism to a wife.

"If, on the other hand, the husband explains that this is a
part of him — has been since childhood — and that he cannot change it; if he can relate it to some of the gentleness
and empathy his wife has found desirable in him; if he
assures her that he loves her with all parts of his emotional
self, and that he is not attracted to other men; if he explains
that he wants to share his interest in women's clothing and
other things womanly, and not to compete with her in this
activity; if he shows continuing concern with her needs as well
as his own cross-dressing needs; if he explains that he is not
abandoning the role of the male husband she agreed to marry,
and he invites her to negotiate the times and extent of his
cross-dressing; if he volunteers to help her learn of other TVs
and their wives and how they continue to support and grow
with one another; if he portrays this as a source of joy and
comfort which can help cement their relationship, THEN, perhaps, she will say, 'THANK YOU. I LOVE YOU.'"

— Allison Marsh
"We Love Each Other So"

With such a balanced, thoughtful approach, the wife's response
is likely to be positive. It is excellent, even for the unmarried. In a
subsequent letter, Allison said:

"I know it sounds screwy for someone to write about this
subject after his own marriage has dissolved. But I know
what I went through, and I saw what happened for my lack
of good information. The marriage would have crashed
anyway, but there wouldn't have been so many years of
diminished self-esteem if I had known then what I know

today. Any help I can give to help someone else avoid some of that pain is worthwhile to me."

Here is the reaction of Beverly, the wife of Kaye, a cross-dresser. She doesn't want secrets or fantasy, but she has needs that must be balanced against our desires.

"I am looking for a balanced, real, accepting relationship with my husband and with our CD activities. I want to avoid isolation — and shame ('you're only as sick as your secrets'). I want to avoid the compulsive need to alter reality to fit a fantasy and perpetuate denial. Hey! After all, reality is an incredible adventure that I'm only just beginning to be brave enough to go on. I don't want to neglect the other important values in my life. I need to be safe. I need to be respectful of myself and others. I need to take good care of my body. I don't want to feel that my needs are subordinated to Kaye's needs. I don't want to get so caught up in this that I feel my personal limits are violated or unimportant."

— Beverly B.
"Beyond Coping"

What a healthy outlook. We each have our own needs, problems and circumstances. For my wife, the primary concern was my intention to remain a husband, not to become her girl friend. The second concern was security, not to do anything that would jeopardize our existing lives unnecessarily. By sharing my innermost thoughts, we could deal with the questions. I promised to discuss any desired actions and not to act until we agreed. By applying the Golden Rule, we could both win.

Luanna Rodgers is a psychotherapist, specializing in the gender community. Her comments describe how we can be true to ourselves while developing our unique style of gender expression.

" . . . careful self-disclosures lead to support. Identifying
oneself as a cross-dresser, transgendered individual or transsexual can be frightening, but it is only through coming to
terms with who we are that we can gain further understanding and the support of others. It is far more gratifying and
healing to be loved and accepted by a few people who truly
know us than to hide well from a million. Finding acceptance from others, furthers self-esteem and self-acceptance.

"The work toward developing a positive sense of self and
gender identity is hard, the cost of not doing it harder, and
the rewards immeasurable."

– Luanna Rodgers
"Developing a Positive Gender Identity"

One last viewpoint. I searched for a poem to declare my secret
of transvestism to my family. There are excellent poems, but I wanted
one that was uniquely mine. I adapted it from material in chapter 6. It
describes who I am. It exposes my fears and vulnerability. It shows
my need to be accepted and loved as I am. It appeals for love.

Do You Love Me?

You know me as a person
who has strong spiritual beliefs,
who loves his wife and is committed to his marriage,
who values family and friends,
and who feels that being a grandfather
is one of the greatest experiences of life.

You know me as a person
who loves children and childlike things,
who is sensitive, caring and compassionate,
who believes in personal responsibility,
and who is committed to working hard
and doing a good job.

You know me as a person
who enjoys good food and fine wines
(plus beer, pizza and ice cream),
who brings humor to the workplace and elsewhere,
who works at physical conditioning and enjoys long
distance running,
and who loves animals, especially cats.

You know me as a person who is discovering
a love for theater and the arts,
who is learning to express his enjoyment of decorating,
colors, fabrics and textures,
who wants to be accepted and loved just as he is,
so, do you love me?

What if I take a chance and become vulnerable,
and disclose my story;
will you still love me?

What if society does not accept part of me, but I do;
will you still love me?

What if I need to expose the truth about me,
to be at peace inside;
will you still love me?

What if I told you that I like to shave my legs,
and wear a skirt;
will you still love me?

I am blessed with a wonderful mother, sister and male friend. I decided to use the poem to introduce them to Rachel. In each case, we met where we could talk privately. They were surprised but responded with love. Telling them is the beginning, a good beginning, of a long procedure of them coming to know the real me. I chose them because of the strength of our relationships and their willing-

ness to consider different ideas. Since then I have told the story to
my two brothers, a step son, a nephew and the rest of our family
members, plus many friends. Each has responded positively. One of
my brothers said he had become more aware of stereotyped views
and found that individuals he met didn't match the stereotype. See?
What we say and do does make a difference. My wife and I have
agreed to continue moving carefully by taking one step at a time.

Your Turn

Once you've learned and accepted the truth about yourself,
tell your spouse, significant other, parent or a friend. The timing,
circumstances and method need to be your own, but consider the
long term impact where truth-telling does not occur. What happens if
the relationship is built on deceit? The price of hiding is painfully
high. Everyone needs the love and acceptance that can only come
from candid and supportive relationships. If love and commitment
are present, there is a willingness to work out problems. A nurturing
relationship is a partnership, where both members help each other,
where nothing is off limits, where no problem is out of bounds and
where anything can be handled in a win/win fashion.

By disclosing yourself, you create the potential for trust, caring,
commitment and personal growth. How can someone trust you, if
you do not demonstrate your trust in them? How can someone truly
care for you, if they do not know you? How can someone be committed to you, if they only know the superficial you? How can someone
facilitate your personal growth, if they do not understand you? They
must know you.

Strengthen First?

Perhaps your relationship needs work before discussing this
subject? How do you want your partner to treat you? Whatever you
want for yourself, give that to them first. There are many things you
can do. Your actions will open fresh doors of communication. That
is how the Golden Rule works. However, if your relationship is hav-

ing serious problems, do not divulge your story without first seeking sound, professional advice.

Well?

Suppose you are healthier than you've been lead to believe. How will you ever find out, if you stay in hiding? How will things ever change, if you don't unveil yourself? How can you begin building bridges between the sexes, if you refuse to take any risk? If you want the same intimacy that women want, shouldn't you take a chance and begin to show your true self to them? How else will they come to appreciate you?

The Arabian Proverb describes the kind of friend you need — a true friend who will stand by you in times of difficulty; not one who is only there for the parties. That's the kind of friend you want your wife or partner to be. If a person stops being a friend after you reveal yourself, were they ever really a friend?

There is risk. Only you can decide if the reward is great enough. Only you can decide how and when to act. But don't forget that to be happy and healthy, you need to find a way to —

Share yourself!

Help

> "I am only one; but still I am one.
> I cannot do everything, but still I can do something;
> I will not refuse to do the something I can do."
>
> — Helen Keller

Who, me?

When this journey started, my only interest was to resolve my problems. That's all I was capable of dealing with at that time. As I found people who were willing to help me, I began to feel troubled by my selfishness. I don't know where I would be without the assistance of *Tapestry*, Virginia Prince, Boulton & Park, my wife, Tracy and other correspondents. Each one aided my quest. Each one did what he or she could. They were the therapists who started me on the road to understanding and accepting myself. I had to reach a certain level of self-development before assisting others was possible. Once I reached that level, I felt compelled to help others with similar needs.

My wife urged me to record my ideas. I wanted to wait until I was farther along in my development, because I didn't have all the answers. Then I realized that no one else did either. If I waited until I had all the answers, nothing would ever happen. So even though I was far from an expert I committed to doing the best possible job starting now. Later I would be able to do more.

Sometimes I would think that one person couldn't do much. Then I would remember the movie, *It's A Wonderful Life*. The main character, George Bailey, believed his life to be a failure and wanted to commit suicide. His guardian angel, Clarence, rescued him, and, to demonstrate the value of George's life, the angel allowed him to see how the world would look if he had never been born. The negative changes caused by his absence were startling, and George realized that he wanted to live. Clarence told George that everyone's life touches many other lives, and, if you aren't around to touch them, it leaves a big hole. I was determined to reach out to touch other lives and not leave a hole.

Is There a Need?

Being a cross-dresser is not a character defect. Still, many of us have serious underlying problems – excessive or compulsive behavior, guilt, denial and a host of related issues. Some use clothes and makeup to block out the outside world and suppress their inner selves. Sometimes these actions create desperate people who do desperate things. Almost any gender publication reports tragic stories of addiction, depression, suicide and other destructive activities. The evidence indicates an overwhelming need.

Our focus has been on the visible gender community, but our community resembles an iceberg – only the tip shows. The overwhelming majority of those affected by gender issues are invisible, hidden beneath the surface of society. Many are not even aware that there are respectable gender groups. These hidden people are trapped in an X-rated world dominated by the worst possible stereotypical views. They need assistance more than anyone. Innovative techniques are needed to reach these people. They need to know that there is great hope for themselves and for their future.

How Can We Help?

We can't become psychiatrists and social workers, but we can show that we care. We can become sensitized to their situation. We can help them focus on their problems. We can help them define steps to resolve those problems. We can be a coach, cheer leader and sounding board. We can help them grow and develop. We can encourage them to express their feelings and desires. We can accept them as they are without being judgmental. We can help them to love themselves. We can be a friend. The basic requirement for helping people is to care for their well-being. If we care, we can help.

"I love you . . . For me to love, is to commit myself, freely and without reservation. I am sincerely interested in your happiness and well being. Whatever your needs are, I will try to fulfill them . . . If I give . . . dishonesty, I will receive your distrust . . . I will give you what I need to receive."

— Walter Rinder
Love is an Attitude

There's that Golden Rule again, giving first to others what you need. The television character Davy Crockett was quoted as saying, "Make sure you're right, then go ahead." You can look for clues indicating serious difficulties. By exercising reasonable caution, you can make sure the person gets the appropriate support that he or she needs. If the individual appears unstable, the best action should be to advocate professional aid. A friend would do that.

Reach out to those in need without waiting to be asked. Society often tries to convince you that you are incapable of meaningful action on any important matter. Even though you can't do everything, you can follow Helen Keller's advice and do the things you can. If you don't help, who will? Who else can? The answer is clear —

Shared Vision – An Open Society

Your Personal Style

Help

Share

Acceptance

Golden Rule

Understanding Emotions

Understanding Sexuality

Current Reality – A Closed Society

You must help!

Educate

"Every day, we see evidence of strength in diversity - in the workplace, in sports, in communities. Too often, however, we see differences not as a way to expand our talents, but as something that divides us. If only respect and dignity could replace intolerance.

"History teaches many valuable lessons. But we must also learn to separate ourselves from the past and the prejudices that define those times. The best way to face tomorrow is with an open mind and an open heart."

— Stephen M. Wolf
"Halting the Hatred"

We Have Rights

The previous steps focused on ourselves, our loved ones and those within our community. Ultimately the public must find out who we are, so the final step is to educate others. As long as we stay hidden in the closet and play by the existing rules, nothing will change. For us to achieve peace and contentment, we must embrace the concept of fully joining society. Remember, we have the right to pursue happiness, as long as we don't infringe on the rights of others.

> *"We hold these truths to be self-evident, that all men are created equal, that they are endowed by their Creator with certain unalienable rights, that among these are life, liberty, and the pursuit of happiness."*

— The Declaration of Independence

Educating others is difficult, but there is absolutely no substitute. Society isn't going to change on its own. It requires commitment and courage to challenge the status quo. We have the goal of an open, accepting society. We have a solid foundation of understanding to build on. We have the Golden Rule as our primary method to make alterations. We have accepted ourselves and are committed to sharing and helping others. Now the question is —

What Can You Do to Educate Others?

You don't have to create a giant organization with global goals. You don't have to launch a massive project. Major transformations result when a large number of individuals each take small steps. Each of us can take steps that will make a difference.

— Tell someone about your feminine characteristics. Choose the circumstances carefully to control the process.
— Donate a book or magazine that presents transvestism truthfully to your local library. Support one of the programs that already do that.
— Place supportive materials in locations where members of the public will see them. Consider the waiting rooms in medical offices where the patients are often desperate for current reading. You can give them something constructive.
— Instead of trying to pass as a woman, select a situation to appear as a man dressed in a woman's clothes. Shop for women's clothing, and, rather than pretending it's a gift, tell the clerk that the

purchase is for you. It offers opportunities to discuss the issues. Ignorance leads to prejudice. If people see and talk to reasonable men who buy women's clothing, some will modify their views.

— Perhaps you could write a constructive article for a local newspaper or magazine. Publishers are looking for interesting, well-written articles.

— Make a public appearance. There are several organizations with educational programs. Volunteers are needed to appear on radio and television programs. Others are needed to give talks to schools and organizations.

— Attend an event sponsored by one of our organizations. There are events all over the country. You can meet new friends, have a good time and grow personally. Take advantage of their social programs to get out in public and present a positive image.

— Question today's clothing and fashion concepts. If you have contacts in the fashion industry, find a pace-setter to sponsor a new trend in men's fashions.

— If you know a trend-setter in show business, ask them to promote softer clothing for men.

— Challenge people to rethink their assumptions. Could you play the part of a five-year old and keep asking, Why? Why? Why? Why Not? This is one of my favorites.

— Lighten up and reach people with a humorous message. Read Nancy Reynolds Nangeroni from the Society of Crossdressing Hardware Engineers (SCHE). The SCHE name alone should get you in the mood.

— Follow the ideals expressed in *Random Kindness & Senseless Acts of Beauty* by Ann Herbert. Perform a kindness for no reason at all; with no thought of getting anything in return. Through these actions you have the power to change things. It is a marvelous application of the Golden Rule.

— Accept a person's perceptions as reality rather than insisting that he or she is wrong. Work to shift the perception. Teach the truth by showing who you are. Don't dress or act in a way that perpetuates the myth of social misfits and sexual deviants. Don't use militant and aggressive tactics to try to force people to accept you. Those approaches frequently result in a backlash, and people grow less tolerant. Remember the Golden Rule and determine how you would want to be treated if you were outside of our community looking in.

— Many people are embarrassed to check out a library book on transvestites or transsexuals. You could insert notes that identify resources that provide help in gender-related issues. Check periodically and replace any notes that have been taken.

— What else suits you?

Diversity Is Good

We can bring positive, constructive diversity. We have the softness that the world desperately needs. President Bush was right when he said that we needed, "a kinder, gentler nation."

> "There's a paradox at work here: e pluribus unum out of the many, one. Every biologist knows that the evolutionary success of any species depends on the diversity of its gene pool. Diversity is healthy, necessary, and maximizes growth potential. The free expression of one's uniqueness is supposed to be highly valued. Our nation is one of many 'melting pots.' Unfortunately this has usually meant assimilation and homogenization to an extent that the richness and potency of diverse peoples was neutralized. Uniting toward a common cause need not require sacrificing our individuality. We need to acknowledge and emphasize our commonality while encouraging and celebrating our diversity . . . Coincidentally, the rest of the world is in need of this very same healing. It wouldn't hurt if we could help set an example."

> — Holly Boswell
> "Getting It Together"

You Are Only One

One of the hardest lesson for me to learn is that I make a difference. My natural tendency has been to complain about problems but not get involved. As a result, nothing would happen. In recent years I finally quit complaining and got involved. Each time I achieved tangible results. Each success reinforced the message that an individual, me, does make a difference.

It's the power of one, a single person, that brings change. A huge throng makes headlines, but a faceless sea of people doesn't normally touch a person's heart. But when one individual makes a statement, people's attitudes do change. It is easy to group unknown people into a generalized view and not treat them as individuals. You've seen the negative effects of stereotyping blacks, Latinos, women, gays and us. Those stereotypes begin to fail when individuals like you show that you don't fit the pattern.

Suppose you come out of your gender closet to your best friend. Your friend knows you, and knowing you causes the ice of your friend's closed mind to transvestites to begin to crack. That is how the world will become different; because you don't fit the assumed pattern. By not fitting the perceived pattern, you alter your friend's attitude. Maybe it's a small alteration, but it is irrevocable. For your friend the pattern will never be the same, since it won't be easy to transform a friend into a hate object. The "coming out of the closet" by an individual is a powerful thing.

Many people's minds are closed to new ideas, and those closed views are often protected with a shiny, icy surface. But that surface can be a surprisingly thin veneer. It isn't strong enough to hold any substantial pressure. As each of us steps forward, the ice melts a little more. Eventually the protective coating collapses, and new ideas and attitudes flood into the mind. Once they get in, the mind can never be fully closed again. All of the numbers finally come down to one. You may be *only* one, but you are *the* one.

No single action will totally solve the problem. That solution will take a lifetime, but each step will make the situation better. The more steps you take, the faster things will get better. The more of us who are willing to take steps, the faster things will get better.

I have always admired Winston Churchill for his courage and tenacity. I believe that he kept Great Britain alive during World War II by the shear force of his will. But far too often I tend to act like Neville Chamberlain and offer appeasement. Appeasement didn't work for Chamberlain, and it doesn't work for me either. My

— failure to confront (meet face to face)
— undesired behavior (things that I don't like)
— encourages repetition (the actions I don't like keep on happening).

So, I'm learning to change my behavior. I am learning that by confronting face to face the undesired behavior that I don't like, I am discouraging repetition, and the bad actions don't keep happening. I have learned that the education of society is my job. It's your job too. It is the most important job, because it will cause constructive transformations. What will you do to —

Shared Vision – An Open Society

Your Personal Style

Educate
Help
Share
Acceptance
Golden Rule
Understanding Emotions
Understanding Sexuality

Current Reality – A Closed Society

Educate society!

The Beginning

"Honk! Honk! Honk!"

—A Flock of Geese

What Is My Dream?

— that you will find self-understanding and self-acceptance; that you will find the strength to become a whole, unique person; that you will spread the vision by sharing, helping and educating; that you will employ the Golden Rule as the primary means of making changes; and that you will keep these ideas in reasonable balance in your life.

— that you will allow time for many small, reversible steps in your quest.

— that you will turn away from the destructive either/or thinking and seek win/win solutions.

— that you will become your own guru, listening to others but relying on your own judgment to decide what is important.

— that you will join the movement and fly along in V-formation just like a flock of geese.

When you see geese heading south for the winter, consider what scientists have discovered about why they fly that way. As each bird flaps its wings it creates an uplift for the bird immediately following. By flying in a V-formation the flock adds more flying range than if each bird flew on its own. People who share a common direction and sense of community can get where they are going more quickly and easily if they are traveling on the thrust of one another.

When a goose falls out of formation it suddenly feels the drag and resistance of trying to go it alone and quickly gets back into formation to take advantage of the lifting power of the bird in front. If we have as much sense as a goose, we will stay in formation with those who are headed the same direction.

When the head goose gets tired, it rotates back in the wing and another goose flies point. It is sensible to take turns doing demanding jobs whether with people or with geese. Geese honk from behind to encourage those up front to keep up their speed. We should encourage our leaders. When a goose falls out of formation two other geese fall out and follow it down to lend help and protection. They stay with the fallen goose until it is able to fly. Only then do they launch out to catch up with their group. If we have the sense of a goose, we will stand by each other like that.

How Did You Do?

You began by asking, "What's in it for me?" You wanted something of value for your investment of time and money. By promoting health, wholeness and unity for the gender community, this book delivers great value to a serious reader like you. As a result you came to understand and accept your gender feelings and actions better and found ways to help your partner to understand and accept them as well. You received encouragement to help others and obtained a framework and techniques to make changes so the world would be more open to you.

The value you are seeking is in your hands, and these ideas have the power to change the world in ways that will be helpful to you. But it won't happen without you. Your success awaits your personalized, artistic touch to awake and become vibrant, alive and powerful. Whatever your current situation, there is something you can do now that will help achieve the shared vision and your own personal style. Whether you are unconnected to the community, know someone in it or are an integral part of it, the key to achieving any goal is *to start.* Your willingness to start, not the speed at which you travel, is the important factor.

> *"... we are all at different stages of our lives and development. Some of us will try to speed up the process and get caught in the speed trap; others will slow down to smell the roses as they go by. Still others will plod along at a steady pace, and then there are those who are willing to get off from time to time and try to learn about what is going on around them.*
>
> *"So, who is right? No one. Every one. All of us. None of us. No matter how fast you travel, there is always someone ahead of you. And no matter how slow you go, someone is always behind you.*
>
> *"If we take the time to listen and talk to the other travelers, we will find interesting tidbits about ourselves, the road ahead, and maybe even the road behind us. Sometimes we might want to take a detour and go back to see or learn something we missed. This doesn't mean we were stupid or lazy or asleep at the time, it just means that we are open to suggestion and criticism. We can all learn from others' experiences."*

> — Brenda Thomas
> "Reflections"

The Rev. Jesse Jackson popularized the phrase, "I am — somebody." Try thinking of that phrase in a different way.

When you read a report about a physical attack on a transvestite, and you think somebody should do something about it, say to yourself, *I am — somebody.*

When you hear someone put down a transsexual as a social misfit, and you think somebody should do something about it, say to yourself, *I am — somebody.*

When you feel the pain and inner hurt because you can't dress the way you want, and you think somebody should do something about it, say to yourself, *I am — somebody.*

And the day came,
when the risk it took to remain closed in a bud,
became more painful,
than the risk it took to blossom!

Resources

If you are seeking help for gender-related issues, these resources are worth consideration:

American Educational Gender Information Service, Inc. (AEGIS)
P.O. Box 33724
Decatur, GA 30033-0724

Ms. Dallas Denny, MA
Licensed Psychological Examiner (TN)

A professionally managed support group and national, nonprofit clearinghouse for information about gender dysphoria. Referrals to professionals and support groups, and to individuals, following the *Standards of Care*; case management; consulting; speakers service.

Publishes *Chrysalis Quarterly.*

International Foundation for Gender Education (I.F.G.E.)
Box 367
Wayland, MA 01778-0367

Merissa Sherrill Lynn
Founding Director

An educational and service organization designed to serve as a communications medium, outreach device and networking facility for the entire TV/TS Community and those affected by that Community. Publisher of materials relevant to the TV/TS theme. Sponsors of the annual *Coming Together* convention. Serves as an international information and referral clearinghouse, speakers bureau, and "drop-in bookstore" for emergency peer counseling and on-going volunteer work.

Publishes *TV/TS Tapestry Journal.*

Society for the Second Self
Tri-Ess
Box 194
Tulare, CA 93275

Carol Beecroft
Executive Director

A non-profit organization exclusively for heterosexual cross-dressers and their significant others. Provides a correspondence directory, directory of commercial services and chapters throughout the US. Membership and attendance at a local chapter meeting requires an interview with the chapter president or older member to ensure that the applicant is heterosexual and complies with the Tri-Ess code of conduct.

Publishes *Femme Mirror.*

Bibliography

B., Beverly. "Beyond Coping." *Other Voices. Educational TV Channel Newsletter.* ETVC, P.O. Box 426486, San Francisco, CA 94142-6486. 1993.

Boswell, Holly. "Getting It Together." *Chrysalis Quarterly.* P.O. Box 33724, Decatur, GA 30033-0724. 1993.

Buscaglia, Leo. *Living, Loving, & Learning.* Ballantine Books. 201 E. 50th Street, New York, NY 10022. 1982.

Covey, Dr. Stephen R. Excerpts of *The Seven Habits of Highly Effective People* used with permission of Covey Leadership Center, Inc. 3507 N. University Ave. P.O. Box 19008, Provo, Utah, 84604-4479. Phone: (800) 331-7716.

Cresap, Janyne. "Going Public." *Cross Talk.* P.O. Box 944, Woodland Hills, CA 91365. Issue #24. Originally published in *Alpha Bits Newsletter.* Alpha Chapter, Tri-Ess, Box 36091, Los Angeles, CA 90036.

Hatfield, Heather."Denial is the Devil." *When Clothes are not Enough.* P.O. Box 380547, Cambridge, MA 02238. 1992.

Herbert, Anne. *Random Kindness & Senseless Acts of Beauty.* With Margaret M. Pavel. Volcano Press, Inc. P.O. Box 270, Volcano, CA 95689-0270. 1982 and 1993.

Kingma, Daphne Rose. *The Men We Never Knew.* Conari Press. 1144 65th Street, Suite B, Emeryville, CA 94608. 1993.

Marsh, Allison. "We Love Each Other So." *TV/TS Tapestry Journal.* Issue #65. International Foundation for Gender Education. P.O. Box 367, Wayland, MA 01778. 1993.

Nangeroni, Nancy Reynolds. *Building Bridges; Coming Out With A Plumb (Pre-publication Draft).* NINJA DESIGN. 276 Pearl Street #L, Cambridge, MA 02139. 1993.

Rinder, Walter. *Love is an Attitude.* Copyright © 1970 by Walter Rinder. Used by permission of Celestial Arts, P.O. Box 7327, Berkeley, CA 94707.

Rodgers, Luanna. "Developing a Positive Gender Identity." *Educational TV Channel Newsletter.* ETVC, P.O. Box 426486, San Francisco, CA 94142-6486. January/February 1994.

Schwartz, Greg. *Straightjacket.* Aegina Press. 59 Oak Lane. Spring Valley. Huntington, WV 25704. 1993.

Senge, Peter M. *The Fifth Discipline, A Learning Organization.* Doubleday. 666 Fifth Avenue, New York, NY 10103. 1990.

Thomas, Brenda. "Reflections." *The Femme Mirror.* 6804 E, Highway 6 South, #334, Houston, TX 77083. 1993.

von Oech, Roger. *A Whack on the Side of the Head.* Warner Books. 666 Fifth Avenue, New York, NY 10103. 1982.

Weintraub, Howard Evan. "The Bliss of Becoming One." My Gift Is Inside. P.O. Box 21534, Concord, CA 94521. 1992.

Wolf, Stephen M. "Halting the Hatred." United Airlines _HEMI-SPHERES_ Magazine. Pace Communications. 1301 Carolina Street, Greensboro, NC 27401. May, 1993.

The Bliss of Becoming One!
Integrating "Feminine Feelings Into the Male Psyche
Mainstreaming the Gender Community

by Rachel Miller

Copies of *The Bliss of Becoming One!* can be had by

— calling, toll free, 1-800-356-9315, Visa/MC/Amex accepted.

— sending $12.95, plus $3.00 shipping and handling ($15.95 postpaid) , plus applicable sales tax to Rainbow Books, Inc., P. O. Box 430, Highland City, FL 33846-0430, Telephone/Fax (941) 648-4420, e-mail: NAIP@aol.com for a direct-order flyer.

— asking your bookseller for ISBNumber 1-56825-031-2

This entire page, as well as the cover and first page of *The Bliss of Becoming One!*, can be modified to reflect your large-quantity or special purchase. More information on large-quantity or special purchases can be made directly to the Publisher, Betty Wright, at P. O. Box 430, Highland City, FL 33846-0430, Telephone/Fax (941) 648-4420, e-mail: NAIP@aol.com.

Notes

Notes

Notes